ONE DAY A YEAR

THE GERMAN LIST

ONE DAY A YEAR
2001–2011

Christa Wolf

EDITED BY GERHARD WOLF

TRANSLATED BY KATY DERBYSHIRE

LONDON NEW YORK CALCUTTA

This publication has been supported by a grant from
the Goethe-Institut India

Seagull Books, 2017

Originally published in German as *Ein Tag im Jahr im neuen
Jahrhundert*

© Suhrkamp Verlag, Berlin, 2013

First published in English translation by Seagull Books, 2017

English translation © Katy Derbyshire, 2017

ISBN 978 0 85742 427 3

British Library Cataloguing-in-Publication Data
A catalogue record for this book is available from the British
Library.

Typeset in Dante MT Regular by Seagull Books, Calcutta, India
Printed and bound by Maple Press, York, Pennsylvania, USA

Contents

My 27th of September

PREFACE TO *ONE DAY A YEAR, 1960–2000*

How does *life* come about? This is a question that has occupied my mind from an early age. Is life identical to time, which passes inescapably but mysteriously? Time passes while I write this sentence; simultaneously, a tiny piece of my life comes about—and passes. Is life thus made up of countless such microscopic pieces of time? Strange, though, that we can never catch it in the act. It escapes the watching eye and the diligently noting hand, and in the end—at the end of a chapter of one's life, too—has assembled itself behind our backs according to our unspoken needs: more substantial, more significant, more exciting, more meaningful, heavier with stories. Life signifies that it is more than the sum of its moments. More too than the sum of all its days. At some point, unbeknown to us, these everyday moments and days change shape into time lived. Into fate, in the best or worst case. Into a lifetime, in any case.

In 1960, the Moscow newspaper *Izvestia* issued a call to the writers of the world, one that instantly appealed to me—they were to describe one day of that year, the 27th of September, as precisely as possible. It was a relaunch of the 'One Day in the World' project begun by Maxim Gorky in 1935, which had not gone unnoticed but was discontinued at the time. And so I sat down and described my 27th of September 1960.

So far, so good. But why did I then go on to describe the 27th of September 1961? And all the subsequent 27ths of September up to today—for forty-three years, now more than half my adult life? And why can't I stop? I don't know all the reasons behind it but I can name a few of them. First of all, my horror of forgetting, which, as I have noticed, wrenches away particularly the everyday life I value so highly. To where? To oblivion. Transience and futility as the twin sisters of forgetting. Over the years, I have been confronted over and over by this sinister phenomenon. It was this inexorable loss of existence that I wanted to combat by writing—one day of every year, at least, was to be a reliable pillar to support my memory—pure, authentic, described with no artistic intentions; that is, left and surrendered to coincidence. There was no way to control what these coincidental days brought my way, and nor did I want to; thus, apparently trivial days stand alongside 'more interesting' descriptions, and I did not let myself elude the banal, nor stage or even seek out 'significant' matters. I began to await with a certain sense of tension what this day of the year, as I soon called it, would bring me each time. Noting down the details became a sometimes delightful, sometimes inconvenient duty. It also became an exercise in preventing blindness to reality.

What proved more difficult was capturing developments in this way. All these individual daily protocols cannot claim to stand for the forty years from which they were picked out, akin to islands. And yet I did hope that by noting down my findings at certain points, at regular intervals, a kind of diagnosis might result over time—an expression of my desire to understand circumstances and people but primarily myself. I wrote down—often beginning on the same day, usually continuing into the next few days—what I had experienced, thought, felt on that day, memories, associations, but also the news that fascinated me at the time, political events that affected me directly, the state of the nation in which I lived and participated up to 1989, and—impossible to predict—the phenomena of the collapse of the GDR and the transition into another society, a different state. And of course my attitudes, changing sometimes abruptly but more often gradually, to all these complex, complicated events—conflict-laden, full-frontal confrontations. In that sense, these notes are more than mere material; they have become evidence—albeit by no means complete—of my development. I had to resist the temptation to correct previous misjudgements and unjust assessments from my current point of view.

These diary pages are very different from my usual diary, not only in their structure but also in terms of content and through greater thematic confinement and restriction. But they were not meant to be published either, unlike other texts of mine that take the course of a day as an occasion for a prose piece: 'June Afternoon', *Accident: A Day's News*, *What Remains*, 'Wüstenfahrt'—exhibits proving my fascination for the narrative potential in almost any random day. In this case, it required a deliberate decision to publish these notes, in which the 'I' is not an artificial I, presents and surrenders itself unprotected—including to those gazes not guided by understanding and liking.

Why would anyone do such a thing? My experience is that from a certain point on, one which can no longer be identified in retrospect, one begins to see oneself historically; that is, embedded in, tied to one's time. A distance comes about, greater objectivity towards oneself. The self-critically examining eye learns to compare, making it not milder but perhaps slightly more just. One sees how much general matter is contained in even the most personal, and one considers it possible that the reader's need to assess and to judge can be supplemented by self-discovery and, in the best case, self-perception.

Subjectivity remains the most important criterion of the diary. This is a scandal in a time when we are to be drenched in objects and objectified ourselves; even the tide of apparently subjective shameless disclosures with which the media pester us is a coolly calculated element of this world of commodities. I know no other way for us to escape from and counter this coerced objectification, infiltrating our most intimate emotions, than by developing and externalizing our subjectivity, regardless of the emotional effort it may incur. The need to be known, including one's problematic characteristics, one's mistakes and flaws, is the basis of all literature and is also one of the motives behind this book. We shall see whether the time for such a venture has now come.

But the crucial reason for publishing these pages is this—I believe they are a testimony to their time. I see it as a kind of professional obligation to publish them. Our most recent history seems to be at risk of being reduced, even now, to easily manageable formulae. Perhaps messages like these can play a part in keeping opinions on what has happened in flux, re-examining prejudices, dismantling hardened views, recognizing our own experiences and gaining more trust in them, allowing unfamiliar circumstances a little closer to ourselves . . .

I have retained the texts in their authentic form. Slight abbreviations have been made. In a few cases, certain passages had to be removed to protect individuals' privacy.

April 2003

Editor's Note

Christa Wolf continued making notes on her 27th of September, as published in book form in 2003 (*Ein Tag im Jahr. 1960–2000*, translated by Lowell A. Bangerter *as One Day a Year,* published in 2007). Initially, she did so to faithfully record the days for her own understanding of herself, whereby she went against this intention of private use even in the first year, 2001, by reading the manuscript aloud at a meeting of writers in the chancellery held by the then federal chancellor Gerhard Schröder on 23 January 2002 (the text was published in *neue deutsche literatur*, VOL. 543, 2002, and in the collection *Mit anderem Blick*, 2005).

The texts are printed here according to the author's own stipulations, based on the versions available as printouts from her computer; in other words, initially authorized by her to a certain extent. We have deviated from this editorial principle in two cases, in which only the first handwritten and thus unprocessed manuscripts were available. In 2008, Wolf could not note down the day's events immediately because she was incapable of doing so following hospital operations, and later fulfilled her duty of commemorating the day only in a hand-written, uncorrected version. Then in 2011 she no longer had the strength to work. She broke off in the middle of writing on the 27th of September. To provide authentic details of these handwritten manuscripts, they are also printed as facsimiles.

Gerhard Wolf
November 2012

ONE DAY A YEAR

2001–2011

Thursday, 27 September 2001
Berlin

I am woken by a loud voice that says: *A rip in the fabric of time.* I listen to the echo of the voice, delighted at the truth it speaks, before I become aware of where I am; that it is early morning, that I'm lying in bed, and the more reality my consciousness reluctantly permits, the more the feeling of delight wanes. I have learnt that truth does not make us happy, because truth alone has no effect. Intrusively, as if they were part of reality (and they are a part of it), my inner screen fills with the last CNN images I saw after midnight last night, after which I found it hard to get to sleep, although I hadn't neglected to take the two capsules of valerian extract. The channel didn't refrain from using the word *war*: 'America's War against Terrorism'.

At a single stroke, the feelings of tension and fear are back, matching this reality and so often accompanying the beginning of the day throughout my life. The question today, then: Did the Americans carry out their threatened retaliation against Afghanistan—or against anyone else?—last night? I manage to persuade myself it's too early to get up yet, so I put off finding out the answer for a while—not at all like back when the Gulf War began, I remember. Then, I was crouching in front of the TV at four o'clock in the morning and saw what I was supposed to see: the fire preceding the American troops' landing on the Kuwaiti coast. I cried and then read in the newspaper that if I didn't condone this war I was against Israel, only to find out much later that the young woman who had provided the final moral justification for the bombings with her eye-witness report of the Kuwaiti babies murdered by dehumanized Iraqis was the daughter of an employee of Kuwait's embassy in the US, and had never set eyes on a single murdered baby.

So I give myself a reprieve before getting up, and extract from the haphazard piles of books on my small glass bedside table the one that seems most suitable for 'the events'—as they are now called—of the past weeks; that is, what suits them with uncanny precision: *City of God* by E. L. Doctorow, which one could, if one wanted, use—abuse—as one more piece of evidence that there must have long been a premonition of catastrophe in the air for sensitive inhabitants of New York, which drove them to an intensive search for a reason for their fear and moral unrest. 'There may not be much time. If the demographers are right, ten billion people will inhabit the earth by the middle of the coming century. Huge megacities of people all over the planet fighting for its resources. Under those circumstances, the prayers of mankind will sound to heaven as shrieks. And such abuses, shocks, to our hope for what life can be, as to make the twentieth century a paradise lost.'

That twentieth century, I think, to which historians had bid farewell, not even two years ago, with the signum of 'cruellest saeculum in human history', which had only once drawn me directly into one of its catastrophes but had otherwise allowed me to lead a life at one of its most dangerous points of conflict, a life rich in tensions but externally comparatively undisturbed. And so the thoughts machine has kicked off again. I get up and pull back the curtain, a grey day, like all the grey days since the 11th of September.

Gerd is in the kitchen already. Coffee or tea? He asks. Tea. In the bathroom, I immediately press the button on the little black radio. No, there's no war yet. The crusade has not yet begun. The anti-terror coalition's ring around Afghanistan is closing up. The former Soviet republics Turkmenistan, Azerbaijan and Uzbekistan are also part of it. The West, I hear (in other words: the USA) has long had an interest in an undisrupted oil transport through Afghanistan. While I take a shower and get dressed—comfortable clothes because I can stay at home for the time being—I hear that hundreds of thousands of refugees are leaving Afghanistan for Pakistan, or withdrawing to the countryside from the cities threatened with bombings. In both cases they have no food; the UN is warning of a 'humanitarian catastrophe' and appealing for millions to prevent the worst, and I, incorrigible, can't help imagining for a fraction of a second that the countries involved in this future war already accepted as unavoidable, above all the USA, might use half of the billions of dollars that the war will swallow up, not to support their arms industry by creating new demand, but might donate these vast sums to the people threatened by starvation for food, medication, for the reconstruction of their already destroyed country and for bribing their apparently corrupt tribal leaders, thus possibly pulling the rug from under future terrorists . . . Unrealistic? All the worse for reality. At lightning speed, I think, good old 'reality' lapses into the absurd, the boundaries of the narratable seem to be shrinking more and more. That would be something to write about, I think. But what for?

We sit taciturn at the breakfast table. Gerd has made his beloved grains, buckwheat groats, which we first came across in their authentic preparation in Moscow, which we sometimes used to bring home from there and can now buy at every organic food store. We pass the pages of the newspaper across the table with terse comments. Bin Laden, 'the world's most wanted man', has allegedly gone underground, the Taliban claim they can't find him, the USA, it says, has set up its confederation with the 'Northern Alliance' to destroy the Taliban, which has Afghanistan under its heel—particularly the women, who have no rights and are subjected to grotesque punishments if they contravene the laws, which were allegedly derived from the Koran. I scan the news reports, some of them inconceivable only days ago—Putin's appearance before the Bundestag; Hamburg's CDU, which lost 4 per cent in the city elections, sees that as a clear mandate from the electorate to form a government in coalition with Ronald Schill, whose right-wing party achieved almost 20 per cent out of nowhere; the USA turns down NATO's military support; the Germans take over the command of the new Macedonian mission; Peres and Arafat resolve new security cooperation; the DAX, which had plummeted over the past few days, has recovered somewhat. This, I think, is the most important news item, the 'normality' for which the global players aim and that we too, with little interest in the DAX, no doubt ought to wish for, as I ask myself, seeing as we're all in the same boat, like it or not, its course determined by the stock markets. Question mark. Although the return to business as usual, with all the thousands of fates that may be connected to it, is more one of the virtual phenomena that I see all around me and not part of reality, I think.

Because what is 'real', if this word still means anything, is the rip in the fabric of time. I've known that, although I couldn't put it into words as such at the time, since that minute on the afternoon of the 11th of September when, on the TV screen in my editor's office (where we had been working on a text, rudely interrupted by Gerd's call: Turn on the TV!), two planes crashed at a short interval into New York's Twin Towers, and while my mind was still incredulously seeking explanations, my body had already grasped the situation and created that unpleasant aching feeling that always alerts me that something irredeemable, usually terrible is happening and that I will never forget the conditions under which I experience that moment. The beginning of the war in 1939. Fleeing from our hometown in January 1945. The Warsaw Pact troops' invasion of Czechoslovakia in 1968. I would have liked to be spared by history in my old age. How I would have liked to release my grandchildren into a more peaceful century.

I remember that two questions arose within me in a short space of time while I stood in the unfamiliar room, hypnotized by implausible TV images: Is this how the Third World War begins? And: Is this the beginning of the end? I began to work on these questions while I packed up my manuscript and then had to wait a long time for the taxi, which had been held up by an ordinary traffic jam, while the reporters' stunned and agitated voices came over the car radio and the driver, a measured man, to my relief, showed shock and sympathy. These two sentences have accompanied me since then, as statements, as words of doubt, as questions, and they have produced varying answers, none of which is enough for me. I still recall how the faces of my American friends and acquaintances appeared in my mind on that unreal taxi drive and how, looking out of the car window all along, I simultaneously saw the houses, streets and squares of my city through different eyes—as possible targets for mindless destruction.

It is almost ten o'clock when I put the newspaper aside, tidy the kitchen, take the washing out of the washing machine and hang it up in the bathroom, all the tasks that make up the fabric of everyday life and, in their sum, the fabric of time; which bother me every day anew because they allegedly keep me from my 'actual' work, and yet satisfy me every day anew, the older I get—precious everyday life. Once I've made the beds I sit on the edge of the bed and flick through the Doctorow book in search of a particular sentence that finally catches my eye: 'No writer can reproduce the real texture of living life,' I read. As direct and laconic as one could ever wish for. I will note this down now then, with the same grim satisfaction with which a patient would listen to his doctor's hopeless diagnosis. As if I hadn't already known that for years, I say it to myself as my computer warms up. How many years? Impossible to say. Some insights reach you, distributed across time, in homeopathic doses, I think, a sly manoeuvre of the mental defence system so as not to wipe out your ability to work at one fell swoop.

Yet when I came home on that 11th of September and found Gerd in front of the TV, the Twin Towers collapsing over and over, I knew this would bring my ability to work to a halt for an undetermined period. I sat down on the revolving chair at my desk, looked very slowly around my room, all its books, furniture, pictures and appliances feigning permanence, but what still counted?—and my eyes alighted on a postcard, a black-and-white photo that is now on the manuscript stand in front of me. It shows Brecht in New York, sitting on a terrace, smoking a cigar, looking up, the towers of New York rising behind him—those comparatively modest towers that existed in 1946, when Ruth Berlau took the photo: the Empire State Building, for example. I remember thinking, couldn't they have left it at that? Couldn't they have thought of the parable of the Tower of Babel? Of the biblical God's rage at our hubris? Or of Brecht's early lines: 'We have sat, an easy generation / In houses held to be indestructible / (Thus we built those tall boxes on the island of Manhattan / And those thin aerials that amuse the Atlantic swell). // Of these cities will remain what passed through them, the wind!'

Brecht and many other German emigrants, I think—years ago I was able to visit a few old Jewish women in their New York apartments—none of them would have survived if it hadn't been for New York, the city of refugees that took in these Germans too and rescued them from their murderous countrymen, who were cultivating an unprecedented regression into barbarism.

The telephone. C., the secretary of our association for the former Jewish orphanage, as we abbreviate it—the exhibition *Jewish Life in Pankow*, on display in the foyer of the Visitation of Mary Hospital, has been partly sprayed with Nazi slogans and swastikas, she says. The police are there already . . . Here too. The hospital is not even a hundred metres away from us, as the crow flies. It is a plague. A germ that has eaten its way into our brave rich world and is infecting it from within. And here too, I think, one question is asked far too rarely and then only by experts: Why?

Why did it seem to me—precisely sixteen days ago it was—as though those two towers were crashing directly into the empty centre of our civilization, the alleged target of the attack? Everyone appeared to know what our civilization is. I resort to dictionaries. The German *bürgerlich* has also been known as 'civil' since the sixteenth century, I read. And look, Goethe coined the German word for 'civilian'. And 'civilization' is connected with 'refinement', 'ethos': 'The stage of development of human society following subsequent to barbarism.' So it's Greek philosophy, the monotheistic religions, the Enlightenment's belief in reason . . . And what if they had all lost their effectualness in the Occident under the 'terror of the economy' and lived on only as chimera inside us? And have not more and more people sensed that this civilization of ours is hollowed out and empty? Have they not had a greater and greater need to talk about it to one another? Have we not more and more frequently heard the words: it can't go on like this? And couldn't the film and television producers make the most money with films in which terrestrial and extraterrestrial monsters drove this allegedly so highly valued civilization into—previously—inconceivable catastrophes?

Stop, stop! I command myself. Turn to everyday stuff. Does my publishing house want to see the designs for the new book cover? It does. A few sentences to and fro on the telephone—yes, they seem to see 'the situation' similarly. No, they can't quite summon up any real jollity. So I finish the letter to Munich with the three versions of the cover for the new book.

And seeing as I'm dealing with the mail, I write the letter to Professor F. that I've been putting off for a long time, describing the circumstances of Adolf Dresen's death, as he was his doctor for a while. Too many friends have died this year, as though an unknown negative force were depriving more and more people of that tiny excess of energy necessary to stay alive. And we would have needed him of all people, Dresen, especially his ability for merciless analysis. He would have given no quarter. He would have explained precisely why he was against this war too.

There is one positive letter to answer. A professor of German from Nuremberg requests a piece for an anthology, in which she intends to collect statements from various people on a line from Pablo Neruda's *Book of Questions*—'Who shouted with glee when the colour blue was born?' I'm looking forward to writing the piece and I already know how it will end—it must have been none other than an alien, shouting with glee as he watched the Earth, the blue planet, being born.

More work. Business matters. Talking to Maria Sommer about the conditions under which she wants to negotiate a contract with a theatre for me. As always, her vision is clear, determined and well thought out; all I have to do is agree, lean back and rely on her. Nevertheless, I have to spend more and more time and energy on the re-use of earlier work and enquiries from younger people who know nothing of the people we once knew, almost nothing of the background to the events in which we were involved. History often seems to me like a funnel, down which our lives swirl, never to be seen again. A dinosaur feeling.

A horn signal forces me to look out of the window. A block of privately owned apartments is being built on the neighbouring plot after all and the ground is being cleared for it. A megaphone voice orders the nearby residents to stay in their houses and open their windows. There's going to be a detonation. Our janitor, busy in the garden, calls up to us that they've found munitions from the Second World War. Gerd says this is just what he's been expecting. The plot lay unused since 1945, he says, an irreplaceable biotope, and there must have been explosives left behind. So we open the windows, the chief blaster's horn sounds three times, I take a seat on the chair in the hall to be on the safe side, there's a moderate bang and then the horn again—all clear. A couple of workers walk up to a small crater. I can't quite suppress a strange feeling of superiority—the likes of us have seen much bigger craters. I can summon the scene effortlessly—April 1945. Our trek on a country road in Mecklenburg. The planes, very low. The American insignia. The pilot's face a white patch in the cockpit, the bombs scattered in the field. The targeted machine-gun fire. And the farmhand then dead in the ditch in my place. No. Anyone who has experienced it cannot be in favour of war bombing. Cannot disregard the 'collateral damage' that accompanies it. Nor the conviction that the end does not justify all means. Or the knowledge that the bombs are also used to cover up the contradictions in our own countries. In any case, first and foremost, contradiction. There are already reports of teachers being disciplined for not sticking to the official language. So soon? I think. Fear that among all the random nonsense with which the pleasure society has distracted us, the real problems might now emerge, issues the established institutions cannot cope with?

I force myself to write at least a few lines, on this day, of the text that actually ought to be the centre of every day. No writer can reproduce the real texture of living life, Mr Doctorow? Well then, my counter-argument: in this world of commodities that bury everything beneath them, the only remaining point of writing is as self-experiment, cutting, dissecting, anatomizing and exposing the tiniest bronchia of one's own person. An old-fashioned concept, and an explanation for why this lengthy work of writing erects sheer insurmountable hurdles around itself.

Today, though, I'm facing one of the easier exercises —a scene at Woolworth's on Second Street, Santa Monica, where I buy a lamp in a long cardboard box, which I will screw to the dining table in my apartment so I have a light to work by. So I describe how a young black man talks to me in the queue at the checkout and I don't understand his slang, then he presses a pack of candy into my hand and asks me to pay for it, giving me a dollar bill that I don't want to accept at first, but he insists. He just has to run to the bathroom, he says and leaves the store with slow steps. As usual, the act of paying and packing takes an eternity with the untrained sales assistant, and then I stand there waiting. The man doesn't come—has he been playing some kind of trick on me?—then all of a sudden he's behind me. Here you are! Relieved, I hold out his package and the change. The previously surly young man is as if transformed, smiling, beaming, thank you very much, madam! A heartfelt farewell; it seems it was a test, and it seems I passed it, I write.

A commentator on the kitchen radio considers the American president's words, 'Either you are with us, or you are with the terrorists,' sadly, sadly appropriate in these times. Perhaps he doesn't know that critical thinking, once suppressed, is not so easy to switch back on once 'these times' should be over.

C. comes and shows me letters from her and her friends and relatives, urging members of the German government not to send an army contingent into war in Afghanistan. There's nothing more we can do, she says.

In the post is the usual amount of invitations to exhibitions and other events, their abundance having the effect that I tend to stay at home. A letter from UNICEF with the request to round up the monthly donation a little and convert it into euros.

Our friend E. has sent us a page from yesterday's *Tagesspiegel*. Underneath the headline 'Cowardly Thinking', the central column consists of photos of intellectuals, lined up above and alongside one another like a 'Wanted' poster, who are accused of this 'cowardly thinking'. 'Artists and intellectuals resort to anti-American resentments.' Good names are muddied by words cited out of context. All that's missing is their addresses and telephone numbers so that the people's anger can reach them directly. We exchange glances. No comment.

I make the dressing for the salad and Gerd cooks a TV recipe, pasta mixed with spinach and a sauce made of cream, cheese and salmon. Over lunch, we discuss the chances of the various parties and candidates for the Berlin local elections in October. Even now, the opinion polls are predicting fundamentally different voting behaviour in East and West Berlin. In the East, the PDS will probably be the strongest party, at 36 per cent; in the West, the CDU at the same level—a city divided again. If anyone had predicted that eleven years ago . . . But here too, the reasons are barely examined, the ungrateful electorate in the East is usually accused of incomprehensible nostalgia. They say there has been evidence that 'the events of the 11th of September' may have brought East and West Germans 'closer together'. In other words, fervour against the common enemy is supposed to solve the problems of German unification? Unlikely.

Tired. I lie down. Pick up Doctorow again. He doesn't abandon me. He has Sarah Gruen, the New York reformed rabbi, say to her small congregation on the Upper West Side—with whom she studies the 'bible written by people', including the delivery of the Tablets of the Law to Moses—'My sense here, what comes through to me, is the understanding these writers possessed of the morally immense human life. [. . .] The biblical minds who created the Ten Commandments that have structured civilization [. . .] provided the possibility of an ethically conceived life.' Structuring civilization . . . There is something consoling about these words, I think, before I fall asleep. Then I'm once again in a kind of labyrinth of empty rooms leading into one another, half-subterranean, I think. Women I don't know come and go but I am aware that a catastrophe is looming and must be prevented. We instruct one another as to how to go about that. In any case, a rather primitive contraption mounted almost invisibly into one of the smooth walls has to be permanently guarded, best of all by me. When I leave the room on one occasion I pass the instructions on to a younger woman—if the catastrophe threatens to arrive, you have to use a fingernail to turn a small cog, which happens to be identical to the adjustment button on my alarm clock. So I leave the room and find out almost immediately—'the catastrophe' is approaching. I run back in. The young woman is sitting in front of the cog, unhappy, holding up one finger—her fingernail has broken off. She couldn't turn the cog. Now it's too late.

Hmm, says Gerd, a rather arrogant dream, my dear. We lay the table for coffee on the veranda; the B.s are coming from Halberstadt. It has got even gloomier outside; rain has set in. Helmut wants to talk to us about a problem that's troubling him. Accusations have come up against his old teacher Hans Stubbe, the well-known geneticist who set up an institute for crop research after the war in Gatersleben, Saxony-Anhalt, which we knew well and where we also met Professor Stubbe, a man of great achievements for genetics in the GDR. He showed civil courage and managed to counter Lysenko's pseudo-scientific theories of the inheritance of acquired characteristics; I wrote a fairly long portrait of him at the time. There are now posthumous accusations from Western sources that he was involved in stealing seeds from the USSR during the war. Helmut has investigated the material as far as possible and considers the claim untenable. Should he even go into the matter at the celebration of Stubbe's hundredth birthday next year? Or would it be better—on the basis of Stubbe's scientific achievements and his standpoint on the problem of 'the scientist's freedom and responsibility'—to pose the question of the geneticist's right, perhaps even obligation, to intervene into life processes using new research findings, an idea that was taboo until very recently?

Not knowing enough about the subject, I can't give him any useful advice but I lean towards the second option. We arrange to come to Gaterslaben again for the colloquium in honour of Stubbe, and that I will read there again for the first time in many years, in decades, as we work out. We remember our lively, critical discussions on genetics and politics back then, in another life.

As a curiosity, Helmut has brought along copies of a few pages from a new essay by Peter Hacks about Romanticism, in which Hacks claims that the East German 'counter-revolution' in autumn 1989 was 'set in motion by at least two Soviet intelligence services, including by their subordinate forces in the GDR's State Security Service. On the surface, it was convened by artists. [. . .] No worker, no farmer and no manager [had] participated in the abolition of the Socialist Unity Party state.' The writers for their part, including myself through *No Place on Earth*, allegedly prepared this counter-revolution through uninhibited propagation of German Romanticism, and we wanted to trigger it as early as 1976, through our protest against Biermann's expatriation, or so I read. However, 'the government of the GDR did not yet wish to step down at that point and put a stop to the matter.' Bravo. That takes a lot of imagination.

We leave for the Literaturwerkstatt on Maja-kowskiring, for our discussion circle. It's raining hard by now. The lights on either side of the entrance are on. I enter the building with a certain melancholy—today is our last meeting here. The Literaturwerkstatt has to move out in December, taking us along with it. The building had Jewish owners before 1933 and is now administered by the Jewish Claims Conference, which wants to sell it at a price that the Berlin Senate can't pay. We've been coming here once a month for almost ten years. I know most of the people who come streaming in little by little, and they know one another; the atmosphere is familiar, people sit in little groups in their regular seats, more of us than usual, and there seems to be a great need to talk—especially because the subject, set three months ago, is almost overly controversial: 'Rome and America—the sole world powers of their era'.

Peter Bender holds the presentation, sketching how these powers, separated by two millennia and favoured by their geographical positions as peninsulas or islands, adhered to isolationism in a long-standing feeling of their own invulnerability, were then forced by wars to intervene in world events, to extend their power further and further and finally to become the sole major power of their era, until one of them, Rome, perished by its superior might and its inner impotence. Alongside many other incomparable fac-tors between the Roman Empire and the Informal Empire of America are the weapons developed to the highest degree of perfection, with which America seeks to make itself invulnerable and which, in this case at any rate, were eliminated by nineteen men with carpet knives determined to commit suicide. Never has a civilization been as vulnerable as ours, says Bender. Two hundred years of insular security had ended for the USA in a matter of hours, and how the country processes that shock, he says, is of existential importance for all of us.

The discussion, lively as ever, more serious than usual, initially gets caught up in the question of whether it is true that nothing is the same as before the 11th of September. The confrontation with this new challenge, people argue, is taking place according to the old pattern of violence against violence; our behaviour has quickly slipped back into the old grooves. But what alternative is there, others ask; do terrorists understand any other language? I've been waiting for that question. I'm all too familiar with the feeling of being backed up against a wall between false alternatives and only having a choice between wrongs, I know all too well that this is a sure sign that a society is in a fundamental crisis, I say, and that it would be essential not to overlook this signal again and keep going. But where are the societal forces that could force the political and economic establishment to perceive their blind spots, created by their arrogance, self-assuredness and of course their wrongly understood interest, which prevent them from seeing reality and realizing that all of us who profit from the present unjust world order can only survive in the long run if we also take care of the welfare of those who are now suffering under this 'order'?

As the speakers change and the arguments go back and forth, I wonder whether a stranger would still be able to tell—like a few years ago—who here comes from the East and who from the West. I remember how our subjects changed, first the problems of changing political systems, then the structures of the West German institutions, and more and more often issues that affect all of us. Actually, I think, this discussion circle has served its purpose; but my suggestion of ending it when the venue moves out of our domicile of many years does not come at a good moment and is immediately rejected. People don't want to lose the closeness to one another or the openness of our discussions, which they say they don't find anywhere else. We'll decide on it next time.

On the late news bulletin, I find out that the interior minister's first security package has been accepted by the upper house.

In bed in that waking state of tiredness that makes it hard to fall asleep, I read more of Doctorow, my loyal companion throughout this day. I come across a surprising passage, written not by the author himself but by Ludwig Wittgenstein and killing off any tendency for European arrogance, should it have clung on anywhere:

> I will say, posthumously, that Europe is the world's sore affliction, that you in America

who have taken the best that Europe has to offer while hoping to avoid the worst are, in your indigenously American phrase, 'whistling Dixie.' All your God-drenched thinking replicates the religious structures built out of the hallucinatory life of the ancient Near East by European clericists, all your social frictions are the inheritance of colonialist slave-making economies of European businessmen, all your metaphysical conundrums were concocted for you by European intellectuals, and you have now come across the ocean into two world wars conceived by European politicians and so have installed in your republic just the militarist mind-state that has kept our cities burning since the days of Hadrian.

What was it that Ingeborg Bachmann said, a student of Wittgenstein? 'Time deferred until further notice / grows visible on the horizon. / [. . .] Harder days are coming.'

Friday, 27 September 2002

Berlin–Woserin

The day seems to be turning grey, despite friendlier forecasts. Before I get up, a few more glances at Michael Jürgs' Grass biography. The chapter is about the private quarrels after his separation from his first wife, after the failure of his relationship with a Frau Schröder, the time when he came closer to Ute and also to Ingrid Krüger, who then gave birth to Nele. All of it entertaining, of course, for those who don't know him—for a long time we thought Nele was the daughter of Wolf Biermann—but it can only be hurtful for Ute and probably for Ingrid Krüger as well. In this particular case, the biographer is trying, I think, to show off his insider knowledge and takes into account that the text becomes less serious for it.

Following the usual morning rituals, the newspaper. Five days after the ballot with that election night that only brought the decision for the red–green coalition in the early hours of the morning. Headlines: SPD wants to break doctors' cartel; Clark: US pressure on UN correct (the question of whether the

USA will start a war in Iraq at any price, and Schröder's refusal to take part in it, helped swing the election); Iraq–al-Qaeda: lack of evidence; USA: election campaign with Saddam; Westerwelle breaks with Möllemann; eight killed in new Middle East violence; the Green Party's Ströbele won a direct seat; the two SPD members who helped him are to be expelled from the party; when stock markets die—the German Neuer Markt is to be closed; the PDS is moving out of the Bundestag—'Only those who give up have lost.'—genocide indictment against Milošević in The Hague; Israeli rocket attack on Hamas; state prosecutor charges Max Strauß with tax fraud. In the Arts section: longing for national kitsch—the tense relationship between literature and politics in the new Russia; star formation under shock—two competing theories hope to explain the creation of self-illuminating heavenly bodies. In the Berlin supplement: cyclist injured women while passing; German in a suitcase—Education Senator Böger preparing reforms for kinder-gartens and schools; police released hostage—and lost ransom; 48,000 runners expected at Sunday's marathon; public employees may soon go home earlier; moth-infested horse chestnut leaves composted; literature night at the city baths, where Jana will be reading from her book. And so on, and so on.

On the business page, the heads of four managers representing 'the decline of the Neuer Markt' are depicted beneath the heading 'Conmen, Bons Vivants and Rogues'. This is where the really important news is, of course, the news that by and large guides the actions of the politicians on the front pages.

While I operate the washing machine, tidy and wash up, I hear on the radio that the eco tax, or its continuation, is a point of contention in the coalition talks between the SPD and the Greens. A discussion panel talks about how to organize extra tuition after the devastating findings of the PISA study on German school pupils' knowledge levels. I send a fax to the Tubachs in Orinda, who want to come and meet us when they're in Germany in November.

I have one and a half hours left for the text about the day of the year 1965, which I have to transcribe from my diary of the time—the eleventh plenum and my reaction to it slightly later. The emotions of the time are absolutely extinguished and I'm surprised at how radical my insights were even then. People are bound to ask why I stayed in the GDR, even though I saw things so clearly. Apart from my difficulty with changing locations—which my life with its many moves seems to contradict—it was simply the insight, or the view, that the other side was no alternative. *No Place on Earth*—that was my basic feeling from that point on. Do I see it differently now? Was I too critical of West Germany at that time? I don't think so. Although they say nowadays that the capitalism tamed by the welfare state was a different kind to today's predatory capitalism, it has not changed its nature; the creature can merely show itself unchecked and unveiled now.

Gerd and I talk about a possible title for the days of the year. I suggest 'Time Axes' and Gerd says it would have to say beneath that 'One Day of the Year' and the forty dates should be listed on the cover. I continue to doubt in silence whether I ought to release the book, already envisaging the disparaging and horrified criticism, but for now I'm getting the manuscript ready for printing, by the spring, and then we'll see.

A quick meal—pasta, ham, olive oil, cheese, salad.

I lie down, read a little of the *Freitag*, sleep very little. Gerd gets up before me and picks up Anton and Ella Yevtushenko. I look through the post in the meantime, as usual almost only invitations to exhibitions and other events, plus the contract for the reading the day before yesterday at the Kulturhaus Oberschöneweide. (I read 'Wüstenfahrt' and then the discussion afterwards was almost entirely about the time around 1989 again, also about the appeal 'For Our Country'. Frau Herzberg had said a few introductory words about my so-called informant activities; I had the feeling the audience were trapped in that time and still seeking consolation and confirmation.) The woman from the Federal Agency for Civic Education, who sent me the contract—a woman from the West, of course—wrote that she wouldn't have known how to behave in the GDR either (that's the kind of placation I can't stand, but she meant well). A Frau Pötter from Wismar writes that a Fräulein Zerndt lives in Wismar, almost a hundred years old now, who taught English and Geography at the high school in Landsberg that I attended, and who was sometimes asked by Frau Dr Paucksch whether she ought to give 'that Christa' yet another A for her essay . . . I vaguely remember, a rather aged miss comes to mind; we must have had Geography with her. I should send my greetings but she's almost blind, so a book wouldn't be the right thing. It's almost uncanny to imagine that this woman, already elderly (to me) at the time, is still alive.

2.35 p.m., departure for Woserin, to Tinka and Martin's party celebrating their joint hundredth birthday—she's forty-six, he's fifty-four. Lots of traffic, Friday afternoon; people are already leaving the city for their country gardens or further away and there are still plenty of trucks on the roads. Sometimes slow-moving traffic but no jams. Ella, sitting behind me, says there aren't any large empty spaces in Ukraine like the ones to be seen here from the car. Even the tiniest piece of land is leased out and used as a garden there, she says, as people have to grow as much of their own produce as possible because of the poor supply situation and the lack of money. They take buses out of town and cultivate their gardens on the weekends. Ella's family is scattered across the world. She's Jewish, lives in Berlin (for seven years now?), was first in Tinka's OWEN and has now opened up her own agency (or something along those lines), advising immigrants, providing tuition, etc. Her daughter lives in Toronto, Canada. Her grandson couldn't get on there, came to her, then lived with his father in Kharkov for a year and has now gone back to Toronto, is making more of an effort to fit in. Ella was originally a Physics teacher.

Sometimes I sleep a little in the car. Anton has his headphones on for the whole journey and won't be spoken to. I'm always surprised by how similar he looks to Helene now when he ties his hair back. He turned eighteen two days ago—come of age in every sense. Hard to imagine. The weather is cloudy at first but after Wittstock, heading north, the sky clears up—'beautiful weather in Mecklenburg!' We take a break at the last service station before the Hamburg exit, very disappointing, bad dry cake, weak coffee.

In Woserin we're the first of the hundred guests expected. The advance commando, consisting of Tinka, Martin, Helene, Timo and Olaf, has transformed the bottom floor into a walk-though dining and socializing space, with tables and plastic chairs that Timo got delivered on a pickup truck from his father, a hospital administrative director. Gerd's bed has been put in my room but it's otherwise unchanged and a good place of refuge. The organizers are in a good mood. 'No stress!' is the slogan of the day. Tinka with a blonde mop of curls after washing her hair, Helene is the party manager and has 'everything under control', Timo provides unconditional support —the two of them come across as though they'd been together for years. Martin is very much part of the family.

Timo talks about his job as a waiter at the Adlon,
how he was put in a tailcoat and had to serve at a big
dinner straight away, with hardly any instructions.
How heavy the plates are on your arm when the
dome is still over them. How your muscles ache from
it the next day. How another waiter who started three
or four days after him tipped a whole plate over a
woman's suit on his first day and didn't even clean it
up properly . . . He's going to do an extra computer
course now, and then he'll start as an intern for a
design company, where he can learn exactly what he
wants to do.

Guests arrive in dribs and drabs, some by car—
the car park down on the grass grows and grows—
some picked up in Güstrow by Olaf. Uta comes, Olaf's
attractive, practical girlfriend from Potsdam, who
runs a wine store there and caters for large parties,
and who is now thinking of coming to Mecklenburg
to be with Olaf at last and stop having a weekend relationship (because he can't sell his flourishing olive
business—the potential buyer can't get a loan from
the banks. So Olaf is still selling at markets across
northern Germany). Uta could imagine going to
France for a year to learn how to make good cheese
and then becoming a cheese maker in Mecklenburg.
Why shouldn't people here be interested in good
cheese? The two of them have taken on the task of
caring for the guests' culinary needs and will spend
all day in the kitchen, chopping, cooking, shaping a
wealth of exquisite starters and a very good pumpkin

soup, so that we'll end up going without the main course, a mushroom risotto for which we brought along the mushrooms and then cleaned and chopped them.

But we're still on the eve of the party and Tinka has made huge pans of Greek-style chicken soup, which the early guests eat in the big room. I sit with the group of Martin's relatives—we're the oldest, of course. The sister Toni and her husband from Bremen, Inge, the widow of the deceased brother Hans from Rostock (I'm told later of her mourning and the terrible trouble her neighbour is causing her), Ludwig, who's the mayor of Wernigerode and immediately signs me up for a reading next April, Ivo, the brother-in-law from Halle, a retired ear, nose and throat specialist, and Heidi, Martin's sister, with whom I get on well, a big-hearted, warm and natural person. We tell one another how we've spent the past year (I regale my various summer ailments); she talks about converting the house after her mother's death, her son's family moving in, about difficulties with the other son, etc.

A group of 'politicians' stands in the entrance for a while, in the middle Hans Misselwitz, who came later because of a meeting with trade union people that he attended as a representative of the SPD. I hear the words, 'We want to steer the economy in a new direction!' so I join them and ask which direction. The answer—in Lafontaine's direction. We can't stay on this neo-liberal course of the past four years, I'm told.

But does Schröder see it that way too? He thinks so. Around us are friends of Tinka and Martin, mostly from the Peace Circle, either Social Democrats or Greens. They're unanimous in welcoming the coup that Ströbele pulled off—winning a direct seat in the Friedrichshain constituency without the Greens putting him forward there—he's too uncomfortable for his own party. (He took his direct seat from a PDS candidate, which had a major political effect—if the PDS person had been the third from his party to get into the Bundestag, power relations would have shifted so that red and green probably wouldn't have been able to form a coalition and everything would have looked like a Grand Coalition of SPD and CDU, which Günter Gaus would have preferred, incidentally.) People are still telling stories of their election night but I notice how quickly the memory of it is superimposed by the new facts.

We sit with a smaller group of friends from the neighbourhood—Andrea, who tells us about the progress in getting funding for the Kulturscheune Rothen, Carola, the potter, and Katrin, the other potter who bought the small half of the house next door a year ago, which was and still is in a terrible state, there's not even water and Pastor Lange has banned her from getting water from the cemetery, Katrin, who is repairing the house in tiny steps with incredible effort and great bravery and at the same time firing beautiful ceramics in a home-made kiln and taking her work to the markets. She talks about the inconceivable bureaucracy that sets in when you apply for a spot at a market, all the application forms and certification you have to hand in and how much you have to pay for it. All particles of reality I would have known nothing about, were it not for Woserin.

Late in the evening, a rather frazzled younger woman arrives (for me, even forty-year-olds and above are now still 'younger' women), who says that she couldn't find the turn-off for Woserin, ended up in Sternberg and then spent another hour circling the by that point rather dark area. A new neighbour across the road helped her once she'd answered two questions for him—What does she do for a living? She paints. Good or bad pictures? That will have been the landscape architect who's moved here, and the last guest is Birgit Schöne, whom we haven't seen for at least twenty years. Against all expectations—she was always talented, quirky, but we thought she couldn't get things done—she has plenty of jobs as a stage designer, is doing great things and tells us indignantly how the managing director at the Theater unterm Dach removed parts of their apparently very left-leaning set design. She feels like complaining to the mayor about it. Her son, who was very small back then and had serious asthma but was healed by a homeopath, is now living in a shared flat in Prenzlauer Berg, she tells us, where the other members let him live and eat for absolutely nothing, and he has a room for himself where he makes masses of modelling clay figures that are apparently wonderful but he doesn't want to market them because he wants nothing to do with this monetary society and lives in absolute modesty. The others regard him as their 'social case' and see it as their task to help him through.

Someone from Berlin also brings along Barbara Buhl from Cologne, whom we haven't seen for years and who landed at Tegel Airport. We had dealings with her very early on when she wanted to adapt a short story of mine for WDR television, then we saw her after the unfortunate *Eulenspiegel* premiere in Hannover; Tinka has stayed in touch with her. She has brought her daughter Leonie, about ten, who immediately makes friends with another girl, falls in love with the house and the countryside and has to say a wistful farewell two days on. At times there are something like twenty children here, populating the grassy field. Thomas Jeutner from Greifswald, now a pastor in Hamburg, comes with his son; the two of them are a two-man orchestra with drums, harmonica and clarinet. (They perform late the next afternoon when a group of Tinka-and-Martin friends, around a core of Ruth and Hans Misselwitz, Marina Beyer and Gerhard Rein, stage a religious tribunal in front of the house to decide whether Saint Katharina and Saint Martin are to retain their saintly status or be sent back down to earth.)

Ralli, Tinka's first boyfriend, comes with his big black dog Willy; their relationship is one of mutual love and dependency. He hands out small cards he's painted and tells me about his work in an institution for the disabled, which he finds very draining. But once a month he takes part in a workshop based on Family Constellations, something he's very convinced by.

We spend the hours up to midnight in conversation—we're waiting for Tinka's birthday to come. When the clock strikes twelve Ivo comes in with a large tray covered in green crepe paper, surrounded by lighted candles. In a box is a chocolate-coated 100 made of sponge cake. Apart from a set of clothes for Tinka and linen shirts for Martin, our present is a long weekend in Rome. Martin gives Tinka a beautiful necklace with a transparent stone and there are lots of other presents. Timo and Anton take care of the music in the background. There's sparkling wine, of course. The mood bubbles up again. But then we all get tired and go to bed before one.

Saturday, 27 September 2003

Berlin

It's eleven o'clock and I've managed to resist the almost irresistible urge to lie down and sleep after reading the newspaper and tidying the kitchen. The washing had to be hung up, amid bouts of sweating signalling that my cold is still very virulent after all, punctuated by coughing fits that stopped entirely, remarkably enough, when I spent half an hour on the Maischberger show yesterday afternoon, and which began again the moment the mike was switched off.

This is the first 'Day of the Year' since the book with the forty-one days came out. It promises to be relatively successful; in other words, it's selling well so far. And yet I've become resistant to feelings of success, particularly for such reasons. The opposite, in fact—when I got up to go to the toilet last night, the question arose in my mind: Have these notes, if I continue them now, lost their innocence? By means of me exposing them to the eyes of the world? Yes and no, I think. Yes, because now 'the whole world' is looking over my shoulder. No, because I'm determined to creep back into my hiding place with these pages and not to publish them, as a continuation so to speak.

I did go back to sleep, unlike two days ago after the book launch at the Academy of the Arts, which had been more agitating and exhausting than I realized. Dog-tired as I was, I couldn't stop the film spooling in my mind—the huge auditorium, opened up on both sides, 700 people, the applause that refused to end, being together with invited guests in the club room, some of whom advised me to 'enjoy' the experience. I find that hard; I always feel like I'm at the wrong party . . . I remind myself that today will be a day of the kind I like best—no appointments or obligations. I make a mental count of the interviews I've given, under pressure from the publishing house, which wants to present a bestseller to Random House—*Brigitte* magazine, *Der Spiegel*, *Der Tagespiegel*, WDR, *Börsenblatt*, RBB, Maischberger. Many interviews by my standards, too many, and I'm already feeling drained by the same questions over and over and the answers tailored to the public. Still to come are the reading at the Berliner Ensemble on 'German Unity Day' and, bad enough, the book fair. And in-between, the constant worry over whether Gerd will bear up to it all. Since his dizzy spell on the last-but-one day in Ahrenshoop, he hasn't been completely intact—unlike me, having come home relatively well recovered apart from this stupid cold . . .

Waking up in the morning, I don't mention to Gerd that today is the 27th of September (he hasn't noticed yet). He was reading Ulrich Dietzel's notes about his experiences as the last director of the East German Academy of the Arts; very interesting, he says; apparently he dealt most of all with Hermlin. I reach for the book at the top of my pile on the bed-side table—Wolfgang Büscher, *Berlin–Moskau. Eine Reise zu Fuß*—refraining, in a very rare case, from fin-ishing the Marinina crime novel (*Anastasijas achter Fall*), because it's too constructed and routine and rather dull. The journalist's march to Moscow is a good read, though—perhaps rather too literary in style at times—telling touching and almost unbeliev-able stories, for instance about a Polish countess. I had hoped he would pass through Landsberg but he chose the more northerly route via Schwerin, which my father took in the other direction with the prisoners' transport in January 1945 . . . Büscher writes about the soil fertilized by corpses on the Seelow Heights. It occurs to me that the chairwoman of the home-land expellees, Frau Steinbach, was on Sandra Maischberger's show before me and had inscribed herself in the visitors' book with a sentimental poem. She's intent on a monument for the expellees in Berlin—deliberately lacking political instinct, in my opinion. Maischberger says, she wasn't expelled like you were; she was the daughter of a member of the German occupation administration in Poland during the war.

Gerd gets up at eight and I say, Come back here, Karlade! I want to touch him. Neither of us knows where the word 'Karlade' comes from; probably from Thuringia. We used to say it to each other often. Gerd offers to let me sleep until nine but I can't. After showering and dressing I put the laundry in the machine. The headline in the *Berliner Zeitung*: 'Chancellor Forfeiting Authority'. What it refers to is that six SPD members of parliament voted against the health reform, despite major pressure. 'CDU Misses Chance to Oust Chancellor'. On the radio I hear that the SPD dissenters will be given a talking to. Someone has even suggested they surrender their seats. Doesn't the basic law say members of parliament are obliged only to their consciences? GDR Stasi killer commando alleged to have murdered 'traitors' abroad; Manfred Krug has a long interview in *Das Magazin* about what a terrific chap he is all round; the musical *Les Misérables* at the Theater des Westens was the society event of the past evening. A long list of the celebs in the audience. (We were invited too but didn't go, of course, just as we don't go to almost all the events we could go to every day.) Tomorrow is the Berlin marathon again with 35,000 participants, including Volker Schlöndorff; Jürgen Habermas and protesting students open the Adorno conference in Frankfurt.

After a glorious summer that never seemed to end, yesterday was perhaps the last really warm summer day. I won't be going out today because of my cough but I can see the still sunny weather outside, although, as I notice as soon as I open the window, the air has got harsher, and I can see the green trees still almost unyellowed. Another summer over. How many more will there be? That question is always present. We never say it out loud.

Gerd returns from one of his almost daily shopping trips and sees me at the computer. What are you doing? Today's the 27th of September! Ah, good! He says. Then list all the things you've done recently. And describe the thing with Mueller-Stahl.

That 'thing' is a rather high-falutin' project by the Amalienpark Galley, for which Gerd is co-responsible, and the Saavedra bookshop. The gallery is exhibiting pictures and graphic art by Mueller-Stahl and he's to read here on 2 October—in the church, of course, because no other space in Pankow is large enough for him. He was unavailable for days until he called yesterday and got me on the telephone. I asked him what they absolutely had to know—whether he would be reading from the pulpit or from a podium, seated. He wanted to read sitting down and then embroiled me in a conversation about how we sadly didn't meet in LA and how he'd have liked to back me up because of the unfair and shameless campaign against me in Germany at the time. Well, how very nice of him. Later he called Gerd and demanded a higher fee— Grass had got more as well, he claimed. The bookshop and the gallery have no money, of course, and today Frau Saavedra managed to convince him that Grass didn't get more and then even donated his fee to the bookshop. She had a rather sheepish Armin Mueller-Stahl on the phone then. Oh, these divas . . .

Gerd had bought soup vegetables and started off the potato soup I'd requested, unpacked his shopping. He'd brought an *FAZ* with him, presumably expecting to find a review of my book in there. I very much wished that wasn't the case, and fortunately that was how it turned out. I'm always glad when I'm not assaulted by reviews. I'd prefer not to read any at all; there have been a few quite friendly ones but Gerd set aside Meyer-Gosau's piece in *Literaturen* in silence— the text was disingenuous, she wrote. She'd just spoken to me after the reading at the academy; after all these years and all that had happened (she had always panned my books), she wanted to say how much she liked this new book . . .

Oh, none of it's important (I say self-imploringly). What's important is that I've been whirled inside out this year and have no middle any more, no subject preying on my mind and forcing me to write. All the external factors flow in there, into this void. There was recently a plan to write about an author who withdraws from it all and disappears for the rest of the world—because I told Gerd about the fantasy I wish for. You can't do it, he said. But you can write it. It seems to me it would have to be a male author, a burnt-out man who not only can't love any more but also can't feel anything except ambition and envy. *Déformation professionnelle* . . .

There won't be any news of the children and grandchildren today. Annette and Honza are in Sicily, Tinka is going to Barcelona on her birthday tomorrow, young Helene, wide awake and active, is an intern at the Friedrich Ebert Foundation, Anton is preparing for his pre-school-leaving tests and then apparently wants to study evolutionary biology, Benni turned up to a reading recently in a highly stylish outfit, a suit with a waistcoat and tie, which was second-hand and correspondingly weathered at second glance, but otherwise he doesn't seem to know yet what to do with himself, and Jana and Frank are seasoned journalists, sometimes a little too caught up in the professional vortex and its laws. Martin has grown into a veritable co-worker, designed the exterior appearance of my book and above all made the collages included inside it. He came to collect us from Ahrenshoop as well, when Gerd couldn't trust himself to drive the car.

But what's the point of this list? Like the whole of this uninspired text, it lacks a soul . . .

Still, more. Shortly before noon—now, the bell is just ringing—comes a young woman, the daughter of Herr Müller from the Palatinate, who's a doctor and organizes annual cultural events with a group of people. We went along once too, went over to Alsace with him, ate our first *tarte flambée*. He often sends two bottles of Palatinate wine, this time through his daughter Babette, a very likeable, fresh, natural young woman in her mid-twenties, a junior doctor in Friedrichshain. Yes, they have to work a lot, she says, but what's worse is the strict hierarchy; the older doctors don't communicate with them at all, they never discuss the progress of a patient's disease, all they get to hear occasionally is that they, the older ones, worked much harder in their day than the young doctors now. I gave her a copy of *Leibhaftig* and she got me to sign the new book for her mother.

The post has come in the meantime. Invitations that go straight into the paper recycling box. I'm supposed to take part in an INKOTA advisory committee meeting. And be the patron of a Cologne literary festival next year (which I can't do—the festival falls exactly on my 75th birthday). A writer sends me his first work of literature, 'reimagining' what happens after my story 'Cassandra'. Two touchingly amicable letters from Ellen and Jörg Jannings, who were at the Academy event and describe their feelings. And then, as usually now, an autograph request—my address must be on some kind of list worked through by autograph hunters, who usually haven't read a line of my work, of course. I have a sheet of paper for such cases bearing the words: 'Frau Wolf does not give autographs except for in books at her readings.' For some reason, I find these autograph requests insulting.

I'm incredibly tired, coughing, taking all kinds of throat sweets, 'I can't get it off my back,' but staying in bed wouldn't be the right thing either. The potato soup is good and of course every time we make this recipe we think of Frieder Schlotterbeck; oh, there are some people we miss so very much. I can envisage the line of the dead in my mind's eye, Heinrich Böll, Anna Seghers, Aenne and Frieder Schlotterbeck, Max Frisch, Raya and Lev Kopelev, Otl Aicher, Inge

Aicher-Scholl, Efim Etkind, Adolf Dresen, Thomas Brasch—'What a seed!' What a wealth of encounters and impulses, simply of humanity. Do we idealize our memories? Is a substance of humanity really now gone?

A lie down, at last. I accompany the Moscow wanderer almost to Minsk, then I sleep. Once we've both woken up we don't feel like getting up and we go on reading our respective books. He doesn't know what's the matter with me, says Gerd, I made such a good recovery in Ahrenshoop and now it's all gone again. I really ought to be walking on air . . . He knows perfectly well what's 'the matter with me' and I know it too, but I don't have the slightest inclination to discuss it so I gather my strength, get up, make tea, take the *Baumkuchen* cake 'into the big room'; it's delicious when it's so fresh, says Gerd. On television we watch a Black Forest gateau being made, with huge amounts of cream, and then a film from a doctors' series in which Karin Gregorek, who was Peter Hacks' lover, plays a petulant countess with a heart condition who is wooed by the senior doctor and objects to the young count wanting to marry the young house-keeper. Well, what is the world coming to! We say, but we know the answer; we're living in the land of progressing social cutbacks and progressing reaction. Civil liberties have tipped once again into bourgeois 'freedoms'. It's certainly more comfortable to fret along with a countess over the staff's bad manners than to consider the reasons for four million out of work.

It's half past five by the time I get back to chipping away at this text. As nothing really happens today, in terms of the outside world—a call from Karin Kiwus, could we get hold of tickets for the Mueller-Stahl event for her?—I no doubt ought to listen to what my mind has to say. Is this most recent book perhaps really my last? Simply because the friction I experience doesn't affect me deeply enough and therefore doesn't spark anything that might kindle a creative flame? *Leibhaftig* was a second serving; the subject will barely stretch to more. Sometimes I think the time directly around 1989, the investigative commission, all that is something I haven't really processed yet. But here too, there's no idea that might organize the material. A man whose inner conflict ends in death? I suppose I'll have to wait and in the meantime provide help for new in-between books— letters exchanged with Anna Seghers, correspondence with Charlotte Wolff—nothing new at all. Processing existing material. I suppose it's necessary but it doesn't fire the imagination. *City of Angels?* Feels a long way away. I have to take a look at it with fresh eyes. Unproductive times. 'Walking on air?' What nonsense, my dear!

The sun creeps around my workplace at the computer. Someone calls and would love to come at the weekend to get some books signed, but is turned down—what's too much is too much. We start making dinner after seven—the wonderful porcinis from the market with very thin little noodles. Good white wine. While we're eating—'with slurpy pleasure,' as Frieder used to say—Helene calls. She has something unpleasant to tell us. Reading my book, she noticed that the notes under the year 2000 are actually the notes on 1999 and those for 2000 are missing entirely. A moment of shock. Gerd immediately checks, realizes that there were no notes for 1999 and the notes from 2000 have been printed under the wrong date. We call Martin. Can it be corrected in the second print run? We have to talk to the publishers on Monday morning. Martin passes on a few more mistakes he noticed at the reading; some were errors of speaking or hearing, one—that I compare the towers of Cologne Cathedral with 'stalactites' instead of 'stalagmites'— I will leave as it is. Martin says Tinka and he will still be up around midnight when her birthday begins; if I want to call again then . . .

I can't stay awake that long. A crime show where the young kidnapped Romanian woman who lost her memory in between is rescued in the end and can be sent back home. A few minutes of the German Television Awards, at which all the screen faces are gathered in one room and we got a strong sense of incestuousness, a few scraps of sporting events. A longer stretch from an old East German film—*Der Staatsanwalt hat das Wort*, in which a young Rolf Hoppe played a forester, a young Lissy Tempelhof his (wronged) wife and a young Angelika Waller his mistress. Ah, yes. It wasn't nostalgia for the East that arose; more like jollity. All this once existed.

I have to go to bed. I call Tinka. She's packing her suitcase and watching a film, which we look for too but I turn it off when it threatens to get violent. Have a good flight, I say. I can't congratulate her on her birthday yet. Next Sunday we're having brunch together to celebrate all the close family birthdays in her tribe. Where, is up to Helene to find out.

In bed, I read a few more pages of the book, which is still set in Belorussia—in Lukashenko's empire, where people no longer believe things can ever get better. I can't keep it up for long; I have to sleep. Unfortunately, I wake up in the middle of the night, driven out of a dream by strange animal images, and notice after some time that I won't be able to get back to sleep, as so often. Now the conversation with Maischberger does catch up on me, spools in my mind, and I wonder whether I said too much, the wrong things, exposed too much of myself. It would be good if I didn't have to watch the show at all but Gerd won't allow that. I tell myself all those spoken and broadcast words are soon forgotten, but that's not much use to me during the night. Am I still dependent on what other people think of me? Less, I tell myself, much less than before. But still to some extent . . .

It's almost four o'clock. In the end I take a Faustan; they take effect more slowly and they're not as strong as I'd hoped. By half past seven I'm awake again and don't know whether I've slept properly at all. The wanderer in the book is approaching the Russian border. Today is the 28th of September.

Monday, 27 September 2004
Berlin

At half past three in the morning, I wake in the middle of a dream. We, Gerd (who remains out of focus) and I, are walking around in a kind of garden space and know we are to be 'taken away'; why and to where remain unspoken and there are no people anywhere to 'take us away', but something bad is going to happen to us. Our greatest worry—how should we tell 'the others', the children, where we are? We think of one possibility—we could leave behind a flower arrangement that they'd understand. We dig two round holes in the earth and put a large round bouquet of bright yellow flowers in one. Cobalt-blue flowers are to go in the other; for some reason, this colour combination would get our message across. But there are no blue flowers. We find pale lilac blossoms, phlox-like, and I pick one and check whether it would fulfil its purpose. That's where the dream breaks off. It was extremely colourful.

I go to the toilet. Before I manage to get back to sleep a lot of things go through my mind, which I'd rather keep empty. First of all Benni over and over, his illness, this year's big worry. As always when I think of him, I send him healing thoughts. I don't allow myself pessimism, out of self-protection and superstition. Then there's the almost funny situation that my most recent atrial fibrillation prevented us from embarking on our long-planned and thoroughly prepared health cure. We would have spent last night, having arrived by train on Sunday, at the cure clinic in Berchtesgadener Land. Our regret that we couldn't go was remarkably mild, I think. My feeling, almost relieved and suddenly in great need of rest, was—ah, two weeks at home alone with no appointments! And Gerd said, at least I can work in peace (he means preparing for a biography of Carlfriedrich Claus). We undid all the preparations on one morning, seemingly with only a small financial loss. Then finally, the problem of my coming change of publishing house came into my mind. My doubts about whether the public statement we discussed with Thomas Sparr at the Olivenbaum Restaurant on Saturday really ought to be issued before I've finished negotiating terms with Suhrkamp; whether that wouldn't make Klaus Eck from Random House even more stubborn. It didn't look like I'd ever fall back to sleep. Then I did.

Awake again at five thirty, this time in earnest. After some time I picked up Günter Gaus' book from my bedside table—*Widersprüche. Erinnerungen eines konservativen Linken*. Gerd had also started reading, the latest Augstein biography. I had got to the chapter on Wehner. Once again, I had the feeling it's the absolute highlight of the book. I had vivid memories of the evening at Maria Sommer's home last winter, when he read the chapter for us. I was glad we'd praised him full-heartedly, something he urgently needed. On second reading too, this chapter seemed moving in its empathy with a highly contradictory and difficult person, noble and decent. Literary in the good sense—which most of the other chapters aren't—because it is undisguised in showing the author's closeness to Wehner and is not shy of expressing feelings (as the rest of the book is, for the most part). My sadness at the loss of Gaus welled up. He is irreplaceable as a friend, as an eloquent, sometimes rather difficult conversation partner, as a concurrer and counterpart, as a storyteller who taught us to understand the old Federal Republic somewhat better. This book does the same, incidentally—and it substantiates and reinforces what we often experienced of him—that he was at times a 'big fish in a small pond' in the old West Germany, and that he suffered when he couldn't be that any more after unification. Sometimes his vanity shines through almost unrefracted. We knew many of the anecdotes he tells, but the list of the big names he not only knew but also advised, in some cases, clarified his importance before 1990 for me once again. Perhaps he estimates it higher than it was—but never mind. The last chapters, which I read in bed later after a morning nap, talk too much about political machinations for me—including some in which he wasn't involved. He is editor-in-chief of *Der Spiegel* by this point and describes the conditions and quarrels there in too much detail for my taste— all that will soon be forgotten. And then the painful breaking off of the chapter when he is summoned to the Chancellery by Willy Brandt to become the first permanent representative of the Federal Republic in the GDR. He would no doubt have made these two planned chapters the highlight of the book, and they would have assured him a considerable readership in the East. I doubt whether that will be the case as it is, given the current state of the book.

So now the routine after getting up (whereby I secretly check whether the fibrillation might have passed overnight; but I can't tell, you can't feel it in your pulse). Showering, etc. The Innohep injection I have to give myself until the Falithrom tablets have brought my blood coagulation value below 2— whatever that means. A slice of bread with the vegetable spread from the organic food store because I want to lose weight as usual. A cup of tea. My various tablets. On the radio, an interview with the SPD secretary general, Benneter, about the results of yesterday's local elections in North Rhine-Westphalia, where the CDU lost 7 per cent of their votes but the SPD also lost over 2 per cent (with an election turnout of just above 50 per cent!) and arrived at their poorest election result in the history of the Federal Republic. Despite the presenter's single-minded effort, the man will not be moved to regret the situation; on the contrary, he claims to recognize the turning point for the Social Democrats declared by Müntefering, just as the CDU man Rüttgers previously declared an election victory despite the losses. There's no saving them, I think.

Leave a note for C. that we haven't gone to our cure. Take the car to Buch. The sky is overcast, occasional showers, the thermometer shows 13 degrees Celsius. Gerd hasn't eaten because he has to have a blood sample taken. The autobahn is more congested towards Berlin than in our direction. We drive past the clinic, which was built for the big cheeses at the end of the GDR years. Gerd remembers once seeing an ear specialist there after one of his dizzy spells. (He doesn't know that today is the 'day of the year', incidentally; I'm glad of that because I couldn't write anything otherwise.) How often have we taken this route to Buch, how often have we passed through the gate into the grounds dotted with the old clinic buildings? The car park is full as usual and Gerd looks for a space elsewhere while I go ahead to register us. It's not a problem that he's forgotten his chip-card because it was read off once already this quarter. I have to go through the internal ward—where I've had several stays myself—to the next building, 134A, to the lab on the third floor. A pretty assistant takes blood from my left earlobe, which doesn't work to begin with, eliciting humorous comments from her. My Quick value is only a tenth higher than on Friday—1.25—but apparently the tablets only start taking effect after three days at the earliest. We'll be seeing each other often, she says. So we shall. I notice I've got used to the idea.

Gerd is downstairs in the waiting area, having delivered his blood. I sit down outside the door for the ECG and he gets two cappuccinos from the vending machine so I can take my Falithrom tablets. It makes quite a mess because of the foaming drink. The ECG nurse gives me a familiar reception. Of course, she says, she saw what was up with my ECG the other day but she couldn't say anything. She wires me up and switches on the machine. It's still there. Does it sometimes go away on its own? Spontaneous recoveries do happen. But rarely.

Waiting outside Dr Hohmuth's door. It's almost eleven now. We sit on folding chairs in the corridor, where the patients have to parade past us. Almost all elderly and old people, not terribly attractive. Most of the women chunky to fat—like me, too. Unflatteringly dressed as well. And the old married couples— one has the feeling they're bored with one another and with life in general, have developed an almost child-like dependency on each other. How do the others see us?

Dr Hohmuth casts a brief glance at the ECG and a second one at my Quick pass. He spends slightly longer studying my old documents from 2002, when I had this same atrial fibrillation for several weeks and it was interrupted by an electric shock. You seem to have done all right with one Falithrom last time. He wants to know my blood group but the information can't be found. Using a model on a poster on the wall, he explains what is 'fibrillating' in my heart. It's not life-threatening, he says, you can exist with it. Exist, I say. Not live. He grins—Oh yes, you can live too. Do you know Professor Cornu? A French communist who came to the GDR. He worked on Marx and Marxism. He was one of the doctor's regular visitors, spent the last twenty years of his life with this atrial fibrillation. Was very active and lived to ninety-three, apparently. Of course, says the doctor, his heart performance was restricted; I'm not to overtax it but I can certainly presume something of myself. I find the ECG graph rather aesthetically pleasing. Yes, he says, if you ignore the irregularity. He shows me that the heartbeats come irregularly between the separate jags—sometimes four, sometimes three, sometimes two. You can feel that in your pulse, he says, but not the actual fibrillation. Medication is prescribed. My next appointment is on Thursday.

The air outside is wonderfully moist. I breathe it in to the fullest while Gerd fetches the car. I tell him about Professor Cornu. Gerd asks what I want to eat. Vegetables. We decide to drive to the Kaiser's supermarket. We buy vegetables, bread, I choose two lean steaks, quark, half-fat butter and so on. All for only fifty-seven euros—in the organic food store, Gerd says, it would have been much more expensive. Back home, it takes me a long time to get up the stairs—oh yes, my heart performance is restricted!

It's approaching twelve by now. In the post are the usual half-dozen or whole-dozen invitations to exhibitions and other events; the vast majority of the paper goes straight in the recycling box under the cupboard in the hall. An invitation from the Leipzig Book Fair—they want me to present a book by Pierre Radvanyi commemorating his mother Anna Seghers at the 2005 fair, as I've been so supportive of the fair. Last week I wrote a harsh, sad statement for the *Leipziger Volkszeitung* when the book trade organization took the national book award away from the Leipzig Book Fair after only three years, and relocated it to Frankfurt in a different form. Getting ahead of myself (I'm writing this on 28 September)—in the evening I happened to read in the latest booksellers' journal *Börsenblatt*, 'The fact that the book trade organization has not continued the German Book Prize awarded together with its partners in Leipzig has also been interpreted as a political move. Christa Wolf spoke of a deepening of the East–West conflict.' No. I spoke of a lack of political instinct in view of the present situation in Germany (which, however, is characterized by economic and particularly mental drifting apart between the two Germanies). More post—I am requested to take part in a celebration for Imre Kertész's seventy-fifth birthday at the Berliner Ensemble in November. A woman sends me a book that I am supposed not only to sign, but also to inscribe with a quote of her choice. These are the letters that appal me every time anew with their thoughtlessness. The Academy of Arts announces its annual general meeting in October—I won't go this time; once a year will have to suffice.

I call Annette, with some trepidation, and ask how Benni was at the weekend when he stayed with them. Not as bad as the weekend before, she says.

My next call is to the 'healer'. The last time she treated me, my atrial fibrillation had already been diagnosed. You lie on a soft mattress and close your eyes while she sits next to you in the lotus position and draws shapes with her hands above the prone body, which are supposed to guide the energy currents coming out of her hands to the desired places in the desired way. It takes about three quarters of an hour. She told me she'd worked on my heart, it had been very intensive, the energy had had such a strong effect that her hands had hurt. She had given my heart a real massage. She had seen constriction there, and something like cramp. I have to tell her that the atrial fibrillation has unfortunately not been reduced. We arrange a new appointment.

The 'healer' is forty, not a beautiful woman but attractive, slim. Her 'gift' revealed itself to her in a meditation during a sickness of her own; she tried it out on herself and developed it on her own. She says there is so much around us that is not material but is still present, and physics is coming closer and closer to it as well—some things are material, she says, and the same can assume the form of energy. She believes in a kind of reincarnation; she says she often sees phenomena in her clients that don't come from their present lives. She doesn't reject conventional medicine but it seems too crude to her, as a permanent treatment. She doesn't know where she got this gift for transferring energies.

I've always been fascinated by phenomena of this kind, ever since the presentation of mindreading and hypnosis that Herr Wandrey gave at my confirmation. She wants to treat my heart three or four times.

C. has arrived in the meantime, thinking we were at our planned cure and planning to water our plants. I ask her how her developments are progressing—she separated after a few months from the man she'd married head over heels, having known him for a matter of weeks, who soon turned out to be a 'deceitful and violent man'. Now she's pushing through a fast divorce, is constantly at the police station because he demolished the flat and refused to move out, and she had unfortunately set up a joint account with him, etc. She reports on the new flat she's found, thankfully, very nice, not expensive, not even far away from us.

I call Maria Sommer, with whom I haven't been in touch for a long time and who is at the very top of my list. As I thought, she's been through a difficult and very busy time—Richard Hey died, one of her first authors. She visited him often in his last weeks and then had to hold the eulogy at his funeral; it was all very upsetting, she says. (Gerd immediately opens up the encyclopaedia at lunch to track down the titles Hey wrote. We don't know any of them and we suspect he will have been generally forgotten during his lifetime . . .) We assure each other that we must see each other soon, and will call again. I'm glad to have got hold of her at last.

Lunch. The steak fried precisely according to the French cookbook with madeira sauce and steamed mixed vegetables on the side—a wonderful meal. The usual ghastly reports on the kitchen radio—more dead in Iraq after American aerial attacks. When I say, almost out of habit, How will it all end! Gerd replies, The Americans have to experience a new Vietnam there. There are reports on the uncertainty over some of the hostages kidnapped by 'insurgents' or criminal gangs, whose murder has not yet been proved by reliable documents, as with many of the other hostages. Two French journalists, two Italian employees of an aid organization, an Englishman who begged Tony Blair by video to do something for him. The respective heads of state remain stony—there can be no negotiating with hostage-takers, otherwise it would be 'open season'. I try not to put myself in the position of these poor people's relatives—we have even had to watch beheadings of the hostages. On domestic policy, correspondents ridicule the mania among all party chiefs to claim yesterday's election in North Rhine-Westphalia as a victory for themselves.

A call from my GP's surgery, Dr Reich. I appear not to have paid the practice fee from my last visit, after the accident. I say I paid the ten euros in the emergency room of the hospital where the ambulance took me. Ah. She has to find out whether there might be a new regulation, says the receptionist, sometimes they change in the middle of a quarter. Then—No, it's fine, I don't have to pay twice.

Afternoon nap, at last. I feel a very great need for it every day. I take the *Berliner Zeitung* to bed with me, not having read it yet today. Headlines—Losses for CDU and SPD; Hannover leaves conference of cultural ministers; KarstadtQuelle: negotiations started. The corporation is deeply in debt and is planning to cut thousands of jobs in its reorganization. Austria's last emperor beatified; on the third page is a report about an 'entrepreneur' arrested for allegedly being the head of a mafia gang controlling all of Neuruppin; the Israeli secret service has killed one of the most prominent Hamas leaders in Syria; there is a commentary on the extreme right wing's success in the latest elections in Saxony and Brandenburg; Economy Minister Clement expects living standards to draw equal in East and West by 2019; Ankara bans torture and vigilantism; Italy's government criticizes Germany's striving for seat on security council; chaotic aftermath of the hurricane in Florida and Haiti; *Bild am Sonntag* is the first: back to the old spelling (a long-running issue, the new German spelling system, a bungled attempt that has been very expensive); France mourns Françoise Sagan; Völler resigns after twenty-six days as coach at AS Rome; Thomas Brussig has written a new 1989 novel, *Wie es leuchtet*. (In the evening, Gerd reads aloud from a positive review of the novel in the

Freitag, which once again mentions that he made me look ridiculous in his first book, *Helden wie wir*. I've never read the book. Gerd expresses his discomfort that Annette and Honza can be friends with him and Jana and Frank are also on good terms with him. I say, sure, if someone had written about one of our children like he did about me, I wouldn't be on speaking terms with him. But I can understand that he's closer to the next generation than I am, as an author, and why should they have to think of me?)

Germany and Poland are planning a joint working group to ward off damages claims attendant on the Second World War from German and Polish citizens —one of the most important news items for me. I have been horrified by the efforts of the 'Prussian trust' that represents the expellees and makes claims for the return of property and damages. Recently, when we were eating at the Borchardt with Trageiser —our farewell meal—I was confronted with his purely legalistic perspective on the process, another permanent feeling of being disregarded, as an 'expellee'. Was that less the case in the GDR, where there were far fewer differences in wealth than in the West? It's undisputed that the expulsion, like any catastrophe, had a traumatic effect on many people, particularly the older ones, and also that this should be acknowledged. Not all of that can be compensated through insight into historical contexts and necessities, as I attempted for quite some time. But I am unable and unwilling to comprehend that anyone would endanger the relatively normal relations with Poland, which are so eminently important, for the sake of an anticipated personal benefit.

Sleep, my favourite activity, until after four o'clock.

Coffee. A few dry slices of crispbread. It's only now I tell Gerd that today is the 'day of the year'. Oh, yes! He says and immediately starts thinking about what I've experienced today to note down.

I only start on these notes at that point. So now I have to write that I spend two or three hours writing —an overlapping of activity and description. The pain in the tendons of my left arm, which unsettled me at first, even eases as I'm writing; I seem to be getting used to working on my normal computer after the long period with my laptop over the summer.

I print out the first pages shortly before seven. As it often does now, my printer pulls in a whole pile of paper and gets jammed. All that remains of my rescue attempts is a single page, which is caught so firmly in the machine that I can't get it out without fearing it will tear and make everything irretrievably unimprovable. I simply leave everything as it is, turn off the computer and sit down in front of the television (the next morning, I extract the trapped page with ease).

We watch *Großstadtrevier*, a classic. We eat our evening meal while one of the policemen from the station is in the hands of dangerous kidnappers, on his tenth anniversary on the job of all days. Gerd made a kind of almost fat-free Thai soup out of the leftovers of our chicken broth, with coconut milk, lemongrass and ginger, and it tastes wonderful. I permit myself a small glass of red wine—alcohol does have calories but, on the other hand, it's healthy when enjoyed in small measures . . .

News—Brandenburg will have another SPD–CDU coalition government; at least five people died in Iraq in US aerial attacks. Three National Guards were killed by a car bomb. By now we listen to news items like this in silence, without comment. Sometimes I remind myself—although the basic feeling is always present—that this war and the conflict between Israel and Palestine are part of a calamity coming towards us, for which no one knows a repellent, and if they did know it they couldn't use it because of the desolate fanaticism of all those involved.

Then we watch *Deine besten Jahre*, a 'family drama' made by Dominik Graf in 1998 and containing many clichés and inconsistencies, along with superfluous dramatization. Martina Gedeck is much better suited to the role of the cheated widow, though, than to that of Brigitte Reimann, whom she played recently. And after the news magazine we even watch the US thriller *A Perfect Murder*, with Michael Douglas. As I soon realize, I've seen it before but I can't remember 'how it goes on'. Surprisingly, at any rate, and perfectly done. On the side, I flick through the latest *Freitag*, which focuses on the social conflicts in the new Germany ('Wealth is inherited, poverty too') and above all on the more marked division between East and West, due to the poverty gaining ground in the East and the predictable consequences of the 'Hartz-IV' welfare benefits laws, due to the resentment in the West over the continuing transfer of funds to the East, which haven't had the desired effect (because part of them flowed back to the West and part was employed wrongly, as Edgar Most, the East and West banker, never tires of explaining), and not least due to cultural differences. These differences refuse to be ironed out and are based on differing attitudes to private property, among other things. At any rate, there is an interview with Lothar Bisky, whose PDS is now the second-strongest party in Brandenburg, although that doesn't stop Platzeck from working with the CDU again, led by Schönbohm. Furthermore, a small and revealing article, 'Kohl and Köhler'—at a 'carefully shielded election appearance by Kohl in Strausberg on behalf of the Brandenburg CDU' the chancellor of German unity said that he only made his promise of 'blossoming landscapes' in the East in the euphoria of the changes. And further, 'There were also people in leading positions in industry in the West who had no interest in the production firms in the GDR developing.' Instead, some corporate leaders were apparently only interested in the seventeen million consumers in the ex-GDR. They didn't need production capacities because they were available in excess. Köhler, the new federal president, knew everything, according to the newspaper, as Kohl's undersecretary of state in the finance ministry, and went along with almost everything. The journalist writes that he is now sweeping away the reality of the constitution in favour of the strict commandment of the inequivalence of all living conditions.

Whatever the case, those who believed, in the early nineties, that alignment of living conditions between East and West would take a generation, and were laughed at and insulted for it, proved to be hopeless optimists. I am frequently surprised at the indifference with which most politicians accept this development, how little they fear the dangers it harbours, which have announced themselves in the right-wing success in the Brandenburg and Saxony elections. Fingers are pointed at the East again—but are the reasons for this malaise analysed? Oh no. Here as little as elsewhere.

I watch a few news items on *Nachtjournal* and can't help wondering why I don't put my resolution into practice of no longer confronting myself with these awful pictures every day. It's midnight. In bed, I spend quite a while reading the beginning of Barbara Honigmann's book about her mother, *Ein Kapitel aus meinem Leben*. It touches me. Gerd, who has read it already, says, Yet more proof of how many different GDRs we all lived in back then.

And of the fact that the past is not dead.

Tuesday, 27 September 2005

Berlin

Midnight. We're still in front of the TV, watching the Costa-Gavras film *Der Stellvertreter*, based on Hochhuth's play. I pay close attention—at precisely midnight one of the freight trains crosses the screen, returning empty from Auschwitz. Gerstein's fight to have his terrible knowledge heard, the prevarications of all those around him, absolutely incomprehensible from today's standpoint, but also those of the pope, the American ambassador; everyone has his own 'good' reasons either not to believe the messages Gerstein sends or at least not to make them public. Gerstein, who climbs the career ladder to an SS *Hauptsturmbannführer* and is responsible for the delivery of the Zyklon B gas, is able to effect minor sabotage and delays but nothing more than that, while the young Jesuit Riccardo pins a Jewish star to his clothing and joins the transport to Auschwitz. Gerstein, whose story the Americans don't believe, of course, hangs himself in his cell.

The ever-recurring question of how far one can stay in a criminal system to 'prevent the worst', how far one ought to follow one's absolute criteria, to the point of self-sacrifice. The problem of presenting concentration camps and persecution scenes was clear once again; Gavras probably did it as 'well' as possible, and yet I always have a sense of falseness, embarrassment. I think this type of 'material' can only be shown on film in a documentary manner. The country in which Gerstein lives is submerged in a dismal atmosphere, it is a hellish land. I lived there too, and I see many bright remembered images that made their mark on me as a child and that were later overshadowed by a knowledge I did not have at that age. I believe most Germans didn't want to have their 'bright' memories taken away and resisted this admittedly very painful overshadowing their whole lives long. Once again, I think that the Jews cannot possibly want to live together with the Germans now.

I go to bed after one. Gerd is reading Werner Mittenzwei's *Zwielicht* for the second time; I've read it too and as good as completely forgotten it. That's what happens to me with all books now. It drives me crazy, I say, what's the point in reading any more then, but Gerd thinks you always retain something. That might be truest of such texts. Just as I then read one, in the magazine *Gehirn und Geist*—on the problem that neuroscientists have when they find an abnormality in the brain of a test person who has volunteered for their studies. Should they tell him? Get a doctor involved? They're already holding conferences on the issue. I understand the problem, based on my recent experiences. The doctor at the ultrasound scan of my internal organs told me there was something odd about one of my lymph nodes, a vein wasn't where it ought to be and it had to be clarified by a second imaging procedure, it might be nothing at all but he couldn't rule out a carcinoma—causing me four weeks of considerable unsettlement until the second procedure dispelled the suspicion.

And then I was so upset that I imposed black suspicion on a dark mole on my skin and overcame my scruples about showing it to a dermatologist, who allayed all my fears. That was a time when the thought of death was close to me and permanently present.

I switch off the light at half past one.

Before I fall back to sleep after going to the toilet in the night I start thinking about my interview with *Die Zeit*. Formulations go through my mind. Are they watertight? Do they go too far? Do they reveal too much of my thoughts, of myself? Is the whole thing too political? They (Stephan Lebert and Bruno Kammertöns) insisted on a few sentences at the beginning about how I see the outcome of the elections. I said, I see them as a true reflection of the state of the country—in checkmate. And I characterize this society, ultimately, as a society in crisis.

During the night I ask myself, as I always do in such cases, was it necessary to give the interview? To come out from behind my cover? I remember what Lebert said to me the day before yesterday—he thinks that by bringing together the different layers of my life, I have developed an astounding *ars vivendi*. That astounded me. Can an outsider see it that way, from the end? Perhaps if they don't know certain intervals of my life in the GDR.

I wake from a dream. I am to give a testimony for Kurt Stern. It must be in the GDR. I know it's Kurt Stern, although the top of his head is covered over by a strange pointed cap. I wonder why I am supposed to testify for Kurt Stern, him being an old and trusted comrade; it ought to be the other way round. That's the feeling I wake up with. I've been asked to write a foreword for Kurt Stern's diaries from the early months of the war in France, when he was interned with many other Germans, including anti-fascists. Perhaps the dream also expresses my discomfort with being requested as a 'historical witness' more and more often, because we're now among those who still experienced certain events, still knew certain people. I try to resist but I can't deny the facts of the matter.

I'd like to sleep another hour or so in the morning but I don't manage it, so I get up at eight o'clock. It promises to be another very nice day. We've been having the most wonderful late summer weather for more than a week, while Hurricane Katrina was followed by Hurricane Rita, wreaking damage along the south coast of America—not quite as bad as was feared, I hear on the radio. I hear that VW has agreed to build the new SUV in Germany after all and not in Portugal; the management used the threat to black-mail the trade union and now they seem to have made concessions. But Samsung wants to cut a large number of jobs in Germany. Later, Bärbel Höhn from the Greens makes a statement on Joschka Fischer's exit from party politics and the applications of four Green politicians as parliamentary party leader. In New Orleans, people from certain areas now free from water have been allowed back into the city. The stock exchanges reacted to the merger of VW and Porsche with losses on Porsche shares.

A short exchange with Gerd before breakfast—shall I make scrambled egg with only one yoke and two whites? I think that's not enough yolk, he thinks it's just right. So that's how I do it. I eat a slice of dark bread with my egg, grated apple and flakes. My usual handful of tablets. Tea.

The newspaper title page has a picture of an American woman being carried away by two police-men; she was staging a sit-in outside the White House. Her son was killed in Iraq. In the left-hand col-umn, under the headline 'Undiplomatic Admonisher', a photo of Marianne Birthler, who had issued a rather random 'estimate' in the heat of the (election) battle of how many former Stasi informers might be in the Linkspartei parliamentary group, which has grown from two to over fifty MPs. She then had to correct herself. Some, says the newspaper, see her as an 'avenging angel', others as a recalcitrant admonisher.

I think she could deal more sensitively with her highly sensitive material and not give free reign to her dislike. The headline Blueprint for Grand Coalition; that's which way the undecided election outcome is now heading. Porsche takes over twenty per cent of Volkswagen shares; a former SPD city councillor allegedly spied on Willy Brandt; the CDU only wants to start coalition talks with the SPD if Merkel gets the chancellery; Poland has taken a major step to the right in the elections; Hurricane Rita flattened entire towns in the southeast of the USA. These are just a few headlines from the newspaper's politics section. I shall leave the other parts aside.

Honza calls. I'd left a message on the answering machine for him the previous evening; he's in the middle of the gruelling editing of his galleys for the book that's finally coming out (*Schornstein*) and is checking the proofreader's edits—that's not easy for him because he writes in German, and while he has a good command of German it doesn't always give him the right answers, intuitively. I talk to him about the page he'd faxed to me, and I've even found an additional error—he says '*der Pflaster*' instead of '*das Pflaster*'.

I busy myself around the flat a little and look out of the window from Gerd's room while he's down having a lively conversation with the property manager, Frau V. I like the way they're standing there; she has her black dog with her, tugging on his red lead; the light falls on them from one side through the still dense green roof of leaves; it feels like a precious moment and I want to remember it. (Later I find out that an architect is moving into the building in the next few days and has also rented the semi-basement flat where the foundation for the elderly used to be, and that a young artist couple are taking the vacant flat on the top floor. That makes the house complete again.)

I sit down at my desk to note down the course of the past few days in my main diary. It's important to me and I realize once again that you forget what you did three days ago if you don't make an obedient note of it every day.

Then I switch on the computer and get down to this text. I actually ought to take my manuscript for *City of Angels* out of the suitcase at last, in which I brought it here from Woserin two weeks ago; by now it's lying fallow. After an unproductive break due to my various illnesses and complaints in the first half of the year, after a polite but harsh critique of the present version from G., after I'd recovered well in Woserin (apart from terribly increasing osteoarthritis in my knee that pretty much lames me), after I had to wait to find a new access point to the text, the material began working within me again, and I hope I've found a good tone, a more confident narrative approach, for which I apparently needed all these years and the hundreds of manuscript pages already in existence. Here in Berlin there have been only distractions, doctors' appointments, post, not least the interview with *Die Zeit*, which cost me a great deal of time. Once again, I found out I have to edit a vast amount, that I can't usually leave the more lax speech as it is, that my better ideas simply come after the fact. It's annoying spending time doing that!

A young woman calls—I can't stop myself from answering the phone!—and says she's ordered a new copy of one of my books because her old one, which had my autograph in it, fell into water. Could she send me the new one to sign? How I hate this habit of sending me books to sign unannounced! This young woman, who seems very nice, at least asks in advance, and I put her off until my reading in Marbach, which is very convenient for her as she lives in Stuttgart.

Gerd, back from the market, waves a large, fragrant bouquet of fresh mint that he bought along with other fresh herbs from his herb man—he's always glad to see him coming, says Gerd, just like the potato woman from whom he bought other vegetables as well—you can't buy only potatoes from her and then go to another stall for vegetables! Yes you can, I say. He says no. I say, You're just a decent shopper. He immediately sets about making minestrone for lunch. He hands me a wonderfully crunchy garlic-pickled gherkin and I sit at the kitchen table, admiring all the magnificence from the market around me, eating my gherkin and feeling happy. There can be no better feeling than this.

And then Tinka calls as well. Amazingly, she is at home for once, back from the Crimea where she and a friend from OWEN held a seminar for women from many corners of the earth, which was very strenuous with a lot of conflicts, but for that reason one of best, she says. She wants to 'come by' tomorrow afternoon, with Martin; later she calls again—Anton wants to come too and grab a piece of cake. They're going to Israel the day after that in a group; she wants to take along two of my books for her friend Lidia there, and she'd be 'pleased as punch if I scribbled my moniker in them'. We toss indecent comments to and fro for a while and then both declare we have to work and have no time for this nonsense, and hang up.

While I'm still at my desk, Ulla Berkéwicz calls from Hanau. She didn't want to let the 27th of September go by without calling me, she says. She wants a mention in the text, in other words. We argue over whether she's a little or a big witch. She's in favour of 'little'. We're on a familiar footing, even more so since her visit to Woserin, where she very much opened up to me—to us. She's taken a couple of days off from the publishing house to write a few speeches that are coming up, and because tomorrow would have been Unseld's birthday. You always think, she says, it's just a day like any other, but then it is a rather different day. I resolve to call her tomorrow.

The minestrone is delicious. Gerd has especially made a very aromatic pesto to go with it with lots of garlic, from a good Italian cookbook, and that's dotted over the soup along with parmesan, and he insists on a 'drink' with it—Campari soda. Gerd made everything with great panache and is glad I'm enthusiastic. Shall I tell you something? I say. I love you. The feeling's mutual, is his dry response.

I put three questions to him that came for me by fax this morning, which the Paris weekly *Courrier International* has asked of fifteen 'personalities' to mark its fifteenth birthday:

1. What was the most important world event in the past fifteen years, in your view? (from November 1990 to today, apart from 11 September 2001)

2. What was the most important event for you personally in the past fifteen years?

3. What will be the most important event in the coming years, in your view?

Gerd wants to say the 11th of September for question one, but that's expressly excluded. The fall of the Wall is before the time period; perhaps the Iraq War is the most important event, or the fact that Germany isn't taking part in it. At any rate something to do with the conflict of 'Christian' culture with Islam. But it's difficult to single out one event—in my personal life, as well; perhaps Benni's illness last year and his (let's hope) continuing recovery. The campaigns against me in the early nineties were also 'important', but they're so long ago now that they don't feel as significant any more.

Here too, I'd rather give various events and developments than a single event. And in the future? I anticipate huge conflicts between rich and poor—in the individual countries and internationally, between rich and poor countries. The conflicts with illegal refugees and with the increasing domestic poverty are only a prelude. We look for positive 'most important events' but don't find any. The lasting most important event in my life is that I have Gerd and our children and grandchildren. The questions smoulder on inside me for the rest of the day. I'm sure I won't answer them for the magazine.

I manage to lie down for half an hour, sleep soundly, get up, get ready to go out and see that there's a call on the answering machine—Kammertöns. He has one more 'teeny-weeny' question and I call him back but he's not there; I ask him to call after four. Off I go with my stick—I can't walk without it any more, and it's difficult enough with it, even the short distance to Kavalierstraße. I'm struggling with this disability, with the pain, but I keep reminding myself that this is the only one of all my complaints from this year that remains. Honza comes towards me, then Annette too, seeming relaxed and not under strain; they're going to the Italian restaurant where they can sit outside in the sunshine. Honza has the cover proposal for his book with him; a figure, he himself, standing on a chimney; I like it. We have to postpone the question about the tenses in one sentence that he wanted to ask me—I have to see the sentence written down. Honza says certain tenses don't exist in Czech grammar and that's why he's uncertain about them in German.

My beautician has put two magazines out for me, copies of *Freundin*, which I flick through while she deals with my feet. She tells me about her holiday in Schlaubetal, where they rented a bungalow by the water—probably a done-up GDR bungalow, she says, it smelled like summer camp; they're going to go back again. This time they only had a long weekend because she wanted her son to be there and he had to go back to school. But they wanted him to spend at least a few days in a different environment, because he and his friends had been attacked by right-wingers the week before, at night in Pankow. He's one of the 'metals' who dress in black but aren't violent. The others were out for violence, started kicking their girls, and then her son called the police; they came quickly and arrested a couple of the right-wingers. Now they're out looking for the person who called the police. He's supposed to make a witness state-ment in court in October, and Frau G. is scared he'll end up on the fascists' blacklist and they'll take their revenge. I'm very upset that all this happened in our nice quiet Pankow.

I find an article in my issue of *Freundin*, listing the respective hormones and other substances respon-sible for particular emotional states and behaviours. On 'being unfaithful'—our body doesn't miss the other person, but the substance PA, which is released in a long-term relationship. We are in a phase in which the neurosciences, in their euphoria about their discoveries of brain activities and substances, are repressing people's responsibility for their own actions. If this one messenger substance is lacking, you can't help being unfaithful. It's not the other person you're missing. (As I write this, I feel anachronistic and moralistic myself.)

Our conversation moves on to the elections. As often in the past few days, I hear from my beautician that she was glad there was no majority for a CDU–FDP coalition. She hints that she voted Green, because they'd done some good things in the past few years and the environment problem is urgent, she says. On the chancellor's TV appearance in the election-night debate, when he seemed absolutely uninhibited, she says he probably must have 'taken something'. But you can tell by that, she says, that all they care about is their own power. I can't remember how we get on to sports, the difficulty of overcoming your 'inner inertia'. Frau G. is having a home visit from a physiotherapist soon, to teach her Pilates; she says she'll ask if she might come to see me as well to do exercises with me, which I can otherwise barely be bothered with.

As always, I enjoy my foot massage and then go over to the cosmetics cabin, lie down comfortably (with a brief exchange on the best pillow, my favoured sleeping position) and have my pre-treatment before the most important part begins—the thorough and deep face and neck massage. As I lie there relaxed afterwards, images and thoughts drift by and once again I remind myself that I've recovered well from several not easy medical interventions this year—the cardioversion for the atrial fibrillation, the implantation of the heart pacemaker, the high blood pressure after that—and that I can be glad and grateful that only this pain in my knee is left, although it's very troublesome. I doze off, get woken up, dress, pay and walk home, again in pain. I wouldn't want to walk longer than these ten minutes.

A fax awaits me from *Die Zeit*; they've cut the piece about Konrad Wolf so much that important parts are missing. I make a long call to Bruno Kammertöns, suggest my own cuts, fax them to Hamburg and it's accepted; the whole thing takes more than an hour.

There's a fax from Honza, the sentence from his book where he had doubts about the tenses. I leave a message on his machine that the sentence is correct.

The post is on the kitchen table—the wonderful thick catalogue from the Carlfriedrich Claus exhibition in Chemnitz, including a very short piece by me, which the museum director praises unduly in a cover letter. A letter from Sonja Hilzinger, whom we proposed for the Caroline Award in Jena, thanking us again and sending her acceptance speech, which I like. A card from the Côte d'Azur, from Sue Stern, who lost her sister in a German concentration camp and had asked me whether Jeanne Stern might have been that sister. Sadly, I had to say no. I had sent her my book and she thanks me in the card. Invitations—to events at the Academy of the Arts, some in the new building on Pariser Platz, which has unfortunately proved rather less than functional. An invitation from the senate chancellery for a function, an invitation from the Staatsoper for a performance of the opera *Salome*. I won't attend any of them; the pain in my knee means I have to avoid even the events I'd really like to go to. For example, I stay away from exhibitions because I can't stand still in front of pictures. I do want to try and improve things through a pain therapist—so that I don't have to face another operation—but sometimes I think I'll have to put up with this state of affairs. Then I'd have to have a stair-lift installed, because going upstairs is a challenge to be feared every time. The children all live on the third or fourth floor; I can't visit them any more.

I have just under an hour, between six and seven, to get back to this text, and then Gerd calls me for dinner. There's a very tasty cocktail made with fresh mint and rum, one of Gerd's famous starter platters that he always enjoys making, and smoked mackerel. This and the hours that follow are the time of day I always look forward to—a time of purely passive consumption.

The television news show has no progress to report between the negotiation partners towards a grand coalition, but it's generally accepted that that's where we're heading. The commentators predict that Schröder will have to step back, possibly also Angela

Merkel. Up to this point, both parties are still insisting on the chancellor's post. In the Middle East, the just cleared Gaza Strip is being bombed by the Israelis again because rockets were fired at them from there. Tinka and Martin are flying to Israel in a group the day after tomorrow . . .

There's a crime show that we get caught up in, even though we actually find it awful, with lots of violence, etc. (I've already forgotten it, as I'm writing this two days later, and I fall asleep in the middle of it, which often happens to me these days, in the manner of old people.) Then later one of the discussion programmes so popular at the moment—'Nationality German; Emotional Life East German'. Four people talk under Herr Stölzl's direction—Jens Bisky, who has just written a very sceptical book on German unity, Katrin Saß, who has become something akin to an expert on GDR issues since her role in *Goodbye, Lenin!*, a Frau Rellin, a journalist from the West who reports about the East, and Lothar de Maizière. It was quite interesting because it showed how strongly the questions of the Germans' 'mental' unity are still present and unsolved—whereby I do wonder how they are ever to be 'solved'. It is now generally acknowledged that 'mistakes' were made in the unification process, that the West Germans and the East Germans did not know each other and even now hardly know each other. The abuse perpetrated with the Stasi files was also mentioned; Katrin Saß said she wanted to see hers straight away and had been spied on the most by her closest friend, which she'd never forget and never forgive; de Maizière said at some point he wants to approach someone from the East based simply on the way they behave now. The main thrust was that the East Germans are gradually finding their confidence again, which had been driven out of them by the West Germans' dominance in the unification process. I ask myself whether we would have believed someone fifteen years ago, had he predicted that these same discussions would still be taking place all these years later. We would have held our heads in despair.

In bed, I read a little more of McEwan's *Saturday*, a book that has garnered a lot of praise recently, being compared to James Joyce and Virginia Woolf because it describes a single day. Well—it's a day in the life of an upper middle-class Englishman, a neurosurgeon. McEwan apparently decided to portray not only his entire life (in flashbacks), but also the current political mindset and worldview of an educated Central European after 11 September 2001. This leads to some elements seeming forced and calculated, and nothing spontaneous. So I read this Henry's detailed recollections of an operation he performed the day before, about which the author has informed himself down to all the medical details, all the specialized terminology. It's magnificent of course, even admirable—but is it necessary? Incidentally, it's the day of the largest mass demonstration in London against the impending Iraq War, on which the protagonist has a divided standpoint because he wants to get rid of the murderer and torturer Saddam. I think of my clear standpoint against that war at the time when it was impending, and of my activities against it. Have we been proved right, looking at the catastrophic situation in Iraq? Or was the situation so catastrophic even then that neither justice nor injustice were possible terms of reference? Is our world in this situation today? Would that be the answer to the question of what will be the most important event in the next fifteen years, in my view? As so often with visions of the future, I think—I won't be here then any more.

I fall asleep quickly.

It is two minutes past midnight and I'm lying in bed, reading the last lines of an essay by Dietmar Dath in the FAZ, 'Science Fiction in Sober Verses', about the literary scholar and poet William Empson, a man I'd never heard of who was born in 1906 and apparently died in the eighties, about whom Dath of course writes knowledgably and intelligently (which I expect of him since reading his most recent book *Dirac* twice this past summer). The lines with which this day thus began, are: '"Whereof one cannot speak, thereof one must be silent"—on the much-quoted closing sentence of Wittgenstein's *Tractatus*, Empson wrote: "The detachment of that phrase from its context is the weakness of our generation. Could Romeo not be written? Were the *Songs and Sonnets* what could not be said? What philosophy cannot state, art lays open."'

I am practising falling asleep quickly; it doesn't work straight away, although I'm very tired. Images of the days in the Rheingau drift past my mind's eye;

particularly pressing are scenes from the opera adaptation of *No Place on Earth*, staged by the Mainz School of Music, a very young woman director who sent the two couples Gunda-Bettine and Savigny-Wedekind prancing across the stage in changing costumes, in this case, in the Brentano Barn, through the audience—partly silly, partly eroticized with no motivation, while Kleist seemed rather imbecilic and Günderrode was embroiled in love affairs. Above the entire performance hung a picture of Honecker, and at one point poor Kleist had to tie a GDR flag around his head all of a sudden. At the end the two of them, Kleist and Günderrode, who hadn't had much to do with each other previously, floated off in a barge-like coffin, Günderrode sporting a bikini decorated with pompoms. Then they were dragged across the stage in body bags by two cleaning ladies, who had no function either. Bettine spent most of the time wearing a super-short dirndl dress.

Later I overheard comments from which I puzzled together what was meant. The cast was supposed to go through three time phases—1804, when the play is set, 1977, when it was written, and 2006, the present. What came out in the end was a pile of manure. The music seemed intelligent, though; the young musician, who resembled Kleist and even had a speech defect like he did, not only seemed talented but also appeared to know what he wants. (A number of reviews have since come out, all far milder and more understanding towards the staging—perhaps we have false expectations because of the book?)

I wake for the first time at five o'clock and remember a short sequence from a longer dream. A likeable younger woman is facing me with one of those metal roasting dishes under her arm, the kind you can use to roast fish or meat in the oven, for example. She says, apparently it's her name, Majewski. I say I have a Polish name too that ends with -ski. I fall back to sleep after some time. When I wake at seven I've unfortunately forgotten the long dream I had; all I see is the face of a young man, of whom I know that he is to be fed well in our home. (I can still see them both, the dream woman and the dream man, on the afternoon of the next day as I'm making these notes.)

At 7.30, earlier than usual, I get up. Check my hair, postpone washing it until the next morning. Shower and so on, the usual morning tasks. Look up in the calendar whether my pain patch is due today— no. Not until Thursday. I remember what I've resolved to do at the beginning of every day, since I often woke up in depressed or fearful moods in Woserin. I tell myself several times a day, in a strong tone, I am doing well, I'm glad of this new day. Incidentally, after a very warm late summer, it seems to be a slightly cooler, in any case overcast day; not unwelcome.

Breakfast. To begin with, my seven tablets as usual, plus one magnesium, one vitamin, one green-lipped mussel (crazy!). Porridge. Frau Bieber comes. There's no time to talk to her today about how she's been doing since last week, about her daughter's operation and her daughter's girlfriend, about the farmhouse they've bought themselves.

News—much agitation over the cancellation of the Mozart opera *Idomeneo* by the director of the Deutsche Oper, Kirsten Harms, who was warned by the criminal police office. At the end of Neuenfels's version of this opera, the severed heads of Prometheus, Jesus, Buddha and Muhammad are brought on stage. Following the bad experiences with the Islamists' escalating protests after the caricatures in a Danish newspaper and the pope's (unfortunate) statement, there is fear—and not only and not in the first place on the part of Frau Harms—of hostility from Islamists. Now no one will admit to having taken the first step, of course. Berlin's interior senator Körting, who had informed the director of an 'anonymous warning', has nothing to do with the opera's cancellation of course, Mayor Wowereit, who knew of the case, finds it wrong; all the artists are clamouring for freedom for art, but no one could have given Frau Harms a guarantee that nothing would happen if the opera had been staged. They are accusing her of coward-liness. I am horrified that we live in a country where her fear is justified, that the Islamists really do exert so much power. By coincidence, today is the start of the Islam Conference convened by Interior Minister Schäuble, at which the matter is also to be discussed.

Gerd fetches the post—an invitation to a reading, which I won't accept, like almost all invitations of its kind. A catalogue from Lands' End. The newsletter from Longo Maï. Advertising for an osteoarthritis remedy that promises miracles and might even sway me, as I'm always hoping to find a remedy that enables me to walk without pain again, but then I read that people with thyroid problems shouldn't take it. The anti-racist 'Gesicht Zeigen!' campaign has sent a reminder of outstanding membership fees.

Dr Bernd Hontschik, with whom we had breakfast on Saturday in Frankfurt am Main, recalls—and reminds me—that when his wife Claudia talked about her work in systemic psychology, which is mainly concerned with positive thinking, I asked whether there is no such thing as tragedy, according to this therapy. They are both still talking about it, H. writes (at some point that morning we had got onto the subject of expectations of death, and Claudia Hontschik said it was actually astounding that older people don't run into the road screaming, in view of the death approaching them so nearby. I could only agree; I feel exactly the same way—'in the Grim Reaper's waiting room'.) He writes in detail about the book series 'medizinHuman', which he edits for Suhrkamp; he would like to include my book *Leibhaftig*. (I don't know whether that would be a good idea.) We, Gerd and I, agree that Honza's *Schornstein* would fit very well into the series and that we'll send it to Hontschik, along with Bovenschen's *Älter werden*—which I had hesitated to do because Claudia Hontschik also has Multiple Sclerosis. (Hontschik: Every time I watch her getting up in the morning it breaks my heart in two.)

A letter from a professor, who reminds me that he had asked me for a signature in *One Day a Year* at breakfast at the Hotel Kronprinz in Greifswald—after the evening event for Wolfgang Koeppen. Now he thanks me for not reacting unkindly and wants to introduce himself. He was a professor of medicine and moved back to his hometown after taking emeritus status. He is writing in such a familiar tone, he says, because reading *One Day a Year* makes the reader a member of the family. What impressed him most, he writes, is how I'd tried 'for decades to balance on the narrow line that an autocratic regime allows between freedom and tyranny'. Utopia can 'never work, because it fails to recognize the banality of human nature'. 'Everything that is social, moral and noble about us, we must work hard for against our instinct-driven nature.' Freud was right, he thinks. At the Hotel Kronprinz he said spontaneously that I had embodied the hope of another GDR for him for decades—I don't remember that, of course, and if it was the case then I don't know at all whether to be glad of it . . . He writes that my confrontation of age, death and dying touches a familiar chord inside him. 'The familiarity with its inescapability, which must never take away one's joy in life, is what gives me genuine freedom from even the last fear.' He thought he recognized something comparable in my diary entries. I really don't know. At any rate, this past summer in particular has taught me that I am by no means free from fear and that death very much holds its horrors for me . . . He also writes in some detail about patients, how differently they receive a cancer diagnosis, and he thinks I have 'learned a lot' in relation to dealing with 'the last things' . . . I really don't know. A long, beautiful letter.

Our midday nap, urgently longed for as ever; we're both always very tired by noon. I have the impression that my head has been spinning slightly less when I lie down than in the past few days. Gerd falls asleep quickly, as always, and I read the *Berliner Zeitung*. Headlines—opera cancellation abhorred nationwide; the director is being left out in the cold; French want many children; Mohammed and the freedom of art; the tipoff (about the alleged threat) came from an anonymous visitor; Franziska Eichstädt-Bohlig most prominent Green politician; the worst one can accuse the director of is having strengthened terrorists' feeling of power; Tony Blair's departure approaching; Health Fund to be topped up; CDU in polls slump; poorly educated teenagers more often pregnant; Tax-Payers' Alliance accuses authorities of wasting thirty billion euro in tax money; associations criticize invitation practice for Islam Conference; Defence Minister Jung plans to withdraw Bundeswehr from Congo at end of November; Bulgaria and Romania allowed to join EU in 2007, but with unprecedented prior conditions; Brazil's president Lula has best chances of re-election; US climate scientist Wallace Broecker sees only one way to avert climate catastrophe through global warming: 'We have to get CO_2 out of the air at a sensible price.' Music lessons encourage brain development; the debate on the anti-doping law is being fought harder than the battle against doping itself; palace demolition is a case for the police; Berlin after the election. The Berlin SPD's committee will decide on its future coalition partner on Friday (Greens or Linkspartei as before, both equally strong); a hotel and new office buildings—competition on urban quarter at the main station decided; docu-drama and patriotic opera in one: Oliver Stone's film *World Trade Center*; neo-Nazis, a report on a dinner outside a cafe disrupted by two cyclists, who passed close by the guests, one belching loudly, the other shouting 'Heil Hitler!' (In the elections fourteen days ago, the NPD got into the state parliament in Mecklenburg Western Pomerania and into several Berlin local councils.) A psychologist examines single people's partner choices using the Quick-Dating Method; ARD television defends moving *Wut* to a later slot, a TV film in which a young violent Turk terrorizes a German family—the television executives fear negative reactions from Turks living in Germany; New Orleans awakens (after the flooding)—football played again in the Superdome. Every day, the newspaper brings it home to us that we are living in a crazy world, drifting towards self-destruction at great acceleration. I am astounded that so few people notice it and that we others who do notice it have grown accustomed to it.

I sleep for three-quarters of an hour and wake with a very clear memory of a strange dream. I'm with Gerd in a neutral room; he raises a cup to his lips and tries to drink, but I see that he doesn't manage it, sinking slowly to one side. I watch this movement with horror and then he collapses. I run to him, shout for help, notice we're actually in a hospital, there must be doctors and nurses, but they pay no attention to me, they walk past, and with the help of a porter I manage to heave Gerd onto a stretcher on wheels and take him into a room, lay him on a bed, calling for help to no avail all the while; a doctor even comes past with several nurses, I recognize him, call him 'Dr Waldeyer'—that was the name of my gynaecologist in Karlshorst in the fifties—but he keeps going with a shrug. Gerd is still in a bad way but he begins to wake up, when suddenly the doctor is with him and my fear ebbs away. I don't tell Gerd about the dream; I'm not quite sure why not.

I read the last of the poetics lectures that Peter Bichsel held in Frankfurt in 1982, which he entitled 'Stories Written by Life'. Literature, he was convinced, is repetition. He then tells a story beginning with the line 'Noldi is a writer,' using it to prove that nothing in the story is invented but it corresponds to the truth at almost no point. With real writers, he tells us, 'the reader will discover that the author is not concerned simply with content, but with reflection, narration and the method of narration. In contrast, trivial writers betray their readers by conveying only content.' I, on the other hand, I think, do consider the content of my writing very important. Too important?

Not so far away from this issue is the view that Imre Kertész expresses, which I hear on the radio while I get changed (we want to go to Tinka's party in the evening). He talks about his most recent book, *Dossier K*, in which he apparently subjects his previous books to an examination by distinguishing and dividing the written from the experienced. This 'What is "true"?' in literature is one of the most mysterious processes in the first place, and the question is no doubt always present with a man as scrupulous as Kertész. He goes as far as saying that there was no way to know whether the hospital barrack in Buchenwald he writes about really existed, until—on the occasion of his Nobel Prize, I think—a man approached him who had lain alongside him in that building and thus confirmed to him, yes, it did exist. And I involuntary think of my fear-ridden manuscript about the City of Angels, which is coming along so slowly, perhaps also because the material, which does seem to be simply 'there', changes year after year and I am not at all certain whether I am catching it in its final, that is, 'true', form. As it is the last important thing I will write, I seem to be asking too much of myself. Giving myself excessive amounts of time without knowing whether I really still have that time. And often, when I see what the young people write,

I ask myself why my writing—the content and contents of this writing—should be 'important'.

We drink tea together, eat half a poppy-seed roll, Gerd's home-made jam. He's very busy preparing his exhibition, which will be on show at the academy and at our gallery in November. It is now almost five o'clock. I sit down at my desk for the first time on this day, but only to cut out the clothes I've ordered for Tinka, which haven't yet arrived, from a fashion magazine and stick them onto a piece of card, which I plan to take to her in place of the real items of clothing. Then the potatoes we put on to cook are done (the old *Hörnchen* variety), and I start to peel them for the Thuringian potato salad we're taking to Tinka's surprise party. (Gerd is busy all day and the previous day with making calls to 'his' Prenzlauer Berg writers to sign them up for various readings he wants to hold on the fringes of his academy exhibition. Adventures with wrong telephone numbers, etc. He is terribly occupied and nervous.) Gerd joins me and mixes the salad with onions, vinegar, oil, pepper, salt, stock—it turns out to be a nice big bowl full.

What I've been putting off for days—I sit down and sign the general contract with Suhrkamp, which has already been signed by Georg Reuchlein from Luchterhand and Ulla Berkéwicz from Suhrkamp, other than me. So now my transfer to the other publishing house is complete—a process with which Luchterhand had great problems and which will probably bring me no material advantages but definitely non-material ones. I don't want to be part of the mammoth Random House corporation; I can use the advantages that the individual parts of Suhrkamp have for reprinting various of my books. And I have friendly relations with Suhrkamp staff—above all Ulla Berkéwicz, with whom we have developed a genuine friendship over a short space of time.

I still have time to make notes on two A4 pages for writing up the 'day', which I'm now working on for the third day in a row. Elke Erb calls—it was very complicated to get hold of her number—she is willing to be part of the readings. She tells me about her trigeminal neuralgia, which she's trying to fight with acupressure, and about how she's supposed to write about Ilse Aichinger but she doesn't know her most recent book, *Unglaubwürdige Reisen*. We promise to send it to her.

We watch the seven o'clock news on TV. Everyone is of the opinion that the Mozart opera ought not to have been cancelled and I'm enraged by the hypocrisy. Then the findings of the latest study on the state of reunification are announced by Minister Tiefensee, who is also minister of transport. So, the 'new states' have no prospect for many years of catching up on the old states in relation to wealth, industrialization, etc. Although more than twenty billion euro has been pumped from the old states to the new ones since 1993. An inconceivable sum, which must surely trigger incomprehension, scorn, even anger in the West, reported without comment in this way. The East simply can't deal with money, they must think. There's no examination of course of how many of these billions have gone to West German companies, flowed back to the West (the renewal of the infrastructure is usually done by West Germans, of course!). And—the fact that the East was first de-industrialized, in the early stages of reunification, not least for reasons of competition. Today, one West German waste disposal man has the entire waste disposal of our region in Mecklenburg-Western Pomerania 'in his hands', and they say that his son has bought the fields of the former farming cooperative, now a limited company. The two of them live in a renovated little palace near to us. The farm workers work from March to October and then register unemployed and are paid by the taxpayer. The lord bribed the people from the village with a party and free beer; now they think he's a 'great gent'.

My pedicurist told me the other day that the time when she was working on a machine in a GDR packaging factory was the best time of her life, because of the solidarity among the workers. But the restrictions! Said a West German when I told him that. He can't get it into his head that the 'little' people are more afraid of unemployment than they used to be of the Stasi. They have managed to knock up a complete oppressive state. They need it urgently; otherwise the way in which unity was 'administered' would be a crime. And all the reports on TV and in the print media about the CIA's former and current crimes can no longer topple this conviction. Apparently, most people in the Western world cannot get it into their skulls that Mr Bush, who kicked off the Iraq War in complete awareness on the basis of lies, is an incomparably worse criminal than the men at the top of the GDR, with their small amount of power, could ever have been. Yet he is still regarded as the respectworthy leader of the Western community of values, of 'freedom and democracy'. And all the while he is nothing but a puppet in the hands of the representatives of the corporations pursuing globalization.

An alarming report—the company running the oldest nuclear power plant in Germany, which was to go off the grid next year or the year after that, has applied to continue operating it. This could be the beginning of the end of Germany's exit from nuclear power, which has actually already been decided. The Greens are up in arms. I resolve to fill in the form for an electricity company that guarantees nuclear-free power, which the people from Ulenkrug Farm gave me. I fail to understand how anyone can be in favour of this—nuclear—power production when still no solution has been found for the permanent disposal of radioactive waste.

Annette arrives after half past seven, without Honza, who has very bad back trouble but did go to court in the morning in Potsdam, where they were convening for the umpteenth time on whether his health insurance company has to pay the costs for the apheresis treatment he's been having for twelve years now. For the second time, the judge ruled that the company has to pay—albeit only from the next quarter on, not retroactively. We'll have to wait and see whether the health insurers will finally bow to this judgement, but it would at least be an immense relief if Annette and Honza didn't have to find four thousand euro a month any more. Annette says they have paid about 100,000 euro for the treatment, with the aid of friends and relatives, in the six years in which the company refused to pay—for a treatment that Honza needs to survive, which the company does not acknowledge because there are no statistical studies on the effects of apheresis—blood cleansing—due to the low number of people suffering from the disease.

I put on my red linen sequinned blouse, which I've never worn before. It's warm enough to go without a jacket, just my thin anorak. Annette has a lovely big leather bag for Tinka, which she can use for folders or a weekend away. It's her fiftieth birthday after all, which everyone is taking slightly more seriously than a usual birthday. We drive to Brunnenstraße together, I climb the three flights of stairs with difficulty, and the surprise is a success—Tinka had no idea about the party Martin secretly arranged; we're the first to arrive and find her sitting on the floor amidst rolls of paper in her newly renovated room. She wanted to tidy up before she went away the next day, to an unknown destination—no one has told her they'll be going to a Pina Bausch show in Wuppertal.

Margit and Malinka come up the stairs with us and Tinka gets an inkling of what's ahead of her,

organized behind her back by Martin. As quick as a
flash, Martin puts two large boards on trestles in the
living room and a long table is created, on which the
new arrivals place the edibles they have brought
along. We deposit our Thuringian potato salad and
smoked pork, two bottles of champagne are uncorked
straight away, Annette has brought ham, Margit a
cheese platter, Hannelore, Tinka's 'boss' at DARE, has
a starter made of thinly sliced beef and rocket, Heike,
Tinka and Martin's flatmate, has made a soljanka
soup under false pretences, Ruth and Hans Misselwitz
come later with pumpkin soup and Joanna, a Polish
colleague from OWEN, brings a dessert. Andrea
comes from Woserin and Jutta Seidel, the dentist, is
there, as is Ute Gölitzer, who lost twenty-eight
pounds last year and gives me the address of her
nutritionist. Apart from Joanna and Heike, we know
all of Tinka's friends. I like the fact that we have a
good relationship with them too, a real enrichment.
To our great pleasure, we find out—rather belatedly,
due to Tinka—that Uta and Olaf in Tarnowitz have
had the baby they so longed for, Luca, and we drink
to their happiness.

Someone suggests that everyone tells the story of
when and how they first met Tinka. I'm the first, of
course, and I say that Gerd was in hospital himself in
Mahlow so I was on my own; I had asked my friend
Rachel over but she was asleep when the contractions
set in at night; I called a taxi, woke my friend and left
the house—the Hungarian uprising was happening at

the same time—for Kaulsdorf, for the clinic, where the bed I was put in and had to lie on for hours was horribly hard; I say that Tinka had of course (!) wrapped her umbilical cord around her neck, that she was born at around ten (or was it more like eleven?) in the morning; sadly, I don't know the exact time for either her or Annette; that the gynaecologist—the same Dr Waldeyer—said, Oh, she's already got one girl!, and was then rather relieved when I welcomed her, once they laid her on my chest, with the words, Hello Little Katrin!

We talk about how some fathers didn't go to visit the hospital if they found out they hadn't had a son, so the nurses weren't allowed to give away the newborns' sex on the telephone. We have to think back to Gerd seeing Tinka a few days later and calling her a 'nose king', having said of Annette that she'd looked peculiar. And Annette remembers that her trauma over her sister was caused by her having to stay with her grandma for a long time so as not to infect the baby with whooping cough, and when she was finally allowed home she was only allowed to look at her little sister with a mask over her mouth, in the pram in the garden, whereupon the baby started screaming. And I can't help thinking of how much I did wrong back then, simply not knowing any better, especially with Annette.

Martin. The first time he saw Tinka was at the photographer Helga Paris's birthday. She caught his eye but she was there with Ralli. They lost sight of each other until they met a year later on the same occasion. Tinka was sitting on the edge of the bed and patted the space next to her, telling him to sit down. The fact that he hesitated, and the face he made as he did so, gave her the idea—it might work out with this one. But he was still with someone else at the time, and on one occasion, she says, all three of them sat together.

Some people met Tinka through Martin and the Peace Circle; Ruth and Hans had come along after they'd declared at the polling station why they wouldn't be voting, and wanted to talk to Martin about what to do next while Tinka was there with him—in this very flat on Brunnenstraße. Ute had been asked by Tinka whether she'd join 'the government'— the women's ministry in the last days of the GDR government, in which Marina was undersecretary of state and Tinka was her assistant. I can't remember Margit's story. Joanna had applied for a job at OWEN and had an interview with Tinka, which she'd been very scared about but it went very well for her. Andrea had met Tinka and Martin in the 'New Forum' group in Mitte—just as all of them, or those who didn't come from the West, had met up in critical circles and groups all the way to underground organizations in the last months and years of the GDR.

Do they mourn their youth, I ask them. They all say no. Jutta says she didn't want to go into politics anyway, she'd always wanted to do what she does now; Andrea says the same. Ruth had just come to

Pankow as a pastor in 1981 when the people from the Peace Circle said to her, Right, this is our church now.

How different, how much more lively, their lives were at around thirty than that same time was for us, for me!

Another bottle of sparkling wine is opened at midnight and we raise our glasses. I realize it's the first time that Tinka and Martin's children haven't been with us. Helene started at the London School of Economics a few days ago and Anton, following a summer internship working on an environmental project on the island of Föhr, is with his girlfriend Jana in a village with an unpronounceable name near Hamburg, just about to come back to Berlin to study Japanese studies (!) at the Freie Universität. We sit together for almost another hour and then we go home, again with Annette. I go to bed very tired at around half past one. It was pretty good actually, says Gerd before he turns to face the wall and falls asleep. I flick through George Steiner's book *Ten (Possible) Reasons for the Sadness of Thought*. I read the motto by Schelling (*Of Human Freedom*, 1809), with which I shall close:

> This is the sadness which adheres to all finite life, which, however, never attains actuality but rather serves for the eternal joy of over-coming. Thence the veil of sadness which is spread over all nature, the deep, unappeasable melancholy of all life.

Only in personality is there life; and all personality rests on a dark foundation, which must, to be sure, also be the foundation of knowledge.

Thursday, 27 September 2007

Berlin

It is six in the evening and I'm now beginning to reconstruct this day, from my notes. It is discernible that it is dominated by a central theme that was struck even at midnight, when I watched part of the film *Herr Zwilling und Frau Zuckermann* on television, a documentary I had seen once before but couldn't remember. That happens to me now with almost every book, almost every film—why does one even bother still watching and reading? Herr Zwilling and Frau Zuckermann live in Czernowitz, where Paul Celan also lived, and are among the surviving Jews who returned to their city from the concentration camps. At one point the camera shows a get-together of these people, almost all of them old, a huddle of men in old-fashioned clothes, few women, with serious faces turned in on themselves, without hope, I felt, but it's not my place to say that of them. People from another world, another time. Once, when the whole city was shown from above, spread out across the plain to the east, I had the feeling that was how future generations would discover a lost civilization.

Herr Zwilling is the pessimist of the two; they both have pupils whom they teach (did they used to be teachers? I didn't understand that because I am losing my hearing and often don't understand things while watching television; it's getting worse).

The city's huge Jewish cemetery, the stones set upright side by side. Graves are broken open, the robbers apparently expecting some kind of booty. The graves of the Zwilling and Zuckermann families too. Frau Zuckermann talks about how her family was driven into the ghetto, into a pigsty, how they had to live in the sty and how her father, her mother, her husband and her son died in the space of a few weeks. She caught typhus, lost consciousness, and apparently people must have fed her so that she survived. If someone had told me fifty years ago that Germans would one day come to me and I'd talk to them about it . . . she said. At an event, she sings a Yiddish song in a beautiful soprano.

A school class. Children from Jewish families where they have no idea of their religion any more. The holy days are not celebrated, candles are not lit for the Sabbath. Many want to leave, apparently; the young teacher regrets that very much. Here again, lessons reminiscent of schools here in the fifties.

It was half past twelve and I would have liked to watch more of the film, but there was much more

of it to come and my eyes kept closing. Off to bed.
I like my new pyjamas. I read a book—the theme
continuing—by the Israeli writer Lizzie Doron, *Why
Didn't You Come before the War?* Another one that I've
read before and forgotten. In the days before, I read
her next book, *On the Brink of Something Beautiful*. The
first one seems to be autobiographical—about her
mother Helena, stories about her in a neighbourhood
in the south of Tel Aviv where only Polish emigrant
families live, at least one member of which was in a
camp, like Helena was. How this experience affects
her present life; how it changed people. How they are
almost consumed by longing for their Polish home-
towns. How they cannot help passing on the destruction the camps caused in them to their children.
And how this disrupts the relationship between the
generations—this is described particularly in her
second book, which is less autobiographical. In me,
that feeling of hopelessness again—how shall this ever
be healed, or even anything approaching that? I have
the feeling it is getting worse and worse. But perhaps
that itself, I can't help thinking, is the prerequisite for
it to—well, what?—get 'better'? I don't know.

Every time I have to get up during the night I read
a chapter from Lizzie Doron, then go back to sleep.
Gerd is reading Gumprecht's little book, *'New
Weimar' unter Palmen*, about the fates of the German
emigrants in Los Angeles. I need to read it for the
section I've just got to in my manuscript.

At eight I get up and go to the bathroom before Gerd; it's usually the other way round. Morning rituals, which automatically raise the questions of how much longer? How many more times? On the radio the first news of the day. The junta in Burma has now begun breaking up the demonstrations by the monks and parts of the general public. Nine killed. And we already know one thing—there is no way to intervene from outside; the opposition activists are abandoned to their fate. A UN resolution was vetoed by China. Sanctions, well yes, but retaining power is more important to those in power. Only China could exert any influence. Reactions to the speech to the UN by Chancellor Merkel, insisting on steps against climate change. Most of them statements of respect—she seems to be more talented in her foreign policy than on the domestic front.

I skip the hair wash that's actually due and put on the clothes I've been wearing for days, all out of laziness. I open the window. Fresh, cool air, overcast sky, rain. Autumn. Isolated sections of the otherwise still green trees are beginning to yellow. There are a good few dry leaves on the ground. The opposite side of Amalienpark is still concealed by the leaves on the trees; that's always my test.

Off to breakfast. Gerd has made soft-boiled eggs chopped up in glasses, which I love. He's already engrossed in the newspaper. I have to pop all my pills out of their packaging, shake them out of the plastic pots. Seven for my basic care, all sorts as nutritional supplements—which have no effect, neither on my osteoarthritis pain nor for losing weight, and yet I keep ordering new ones whenever a new blurb comes in the post. And they come in masses.

Gerd reads in the *Berliner Blatt* that thirteen cyclists have been killed so far this year by cars turning right. It's his worst nightmare. Apart from that, Berlin is apparently the city where the most cars are stolen; recently, older models.

A few headlines—protesters killed in Burma; the world in phonetic spelling (which is written into Bush's speeches because he can't pronounce foreign names otherwise. Got blasted out into the world via the Internet.); mood swings before the elections (in Poland); CDU against minimum wage for post deliverers; inheritance tax reform delayed; 5.7 billion euro against AIDS, malaria, TB; Iran's president intends to ignore UN resolution; maintenance after divorce may be time-limited; every fourth child feels ill frequently; desperately seeking teachers (in Berlin); blue tongue disease puts zoos at risk; flat tyres for a better world climate (environmental activists letting air out of car tyres); NPD not coming to Rauen; Hollywood banned from filming in Sachsenhausen concentration camp; Stone Age farmers irrigated their fields; balm for sick joints (a new remedy. Unfortunately it seems to be only for arthritis, not for osteoarthritis. And has to be used early—with me, it's now reached the point where I am reluctant to walk at all and don't even use the new stair-lift to ride downstairs every day and then walk a little.).

In the arts pages—a review of a new film starring Jodie Foster, *The Brave One*, a woman, witness to a murder. Has to defend her life by killing; described as a questionable model. Academy of Arts buys Otto Nagel archive; the heart growing cold; a review of Julia Franck's new novel *The Blind Side of the Heart* (it apparently creates 'illusionary worlds'); distance on all sides: on Peter Merseburger's biography of Augstein, which Gerd is very impressed by; 'Nonsense, I just wanted to get girls'—confessions of Harald Schmidt in *Die Zeit*; another red herring: photo from Morocco not of missing Madeleine.

Unusually, a parcel comes this early—it's only ten o'clock—containing post from Woserin, sent on by Andrea ('Frau Klein'). A letter and poems from Blanche Kommerell, who wrongly thought I was at the convalescence clinic in Ahrenshoop and wishes me a swift return to health; a reader sends a book in which she 'processes her psychoses' and I note with some discomfort that these reports from readers, which are presumably not uninteresting, are beginning to pile up again. And I never get around to reading them and reacting, which the senders of course expect.

To my surprise, although I don't let it show, Gerd has ordered a high-necked white shirt from Walbusch, a kind of dress shirt, and fabric samples that come in a kind of brochure that he has to send back again! He announces he's making 'ragout with vegetables' for lunch, a recipe of his own! He has already got the vegetables out and now he starts to chop and fry the turkey breast.

I walk around the flat, make the beds, open all the windows. From the living room window I see a young blonde woman walking past, in a white jacket and black trousers; I watch enviously as she walks without effort, as if that were the most natural thing in the world.

I console myself—when I was her age I could do that too.

On the sill outside my window are three beautifully shaped yellow linden leaves. It's autumn, I think. A wind blows and the leaves in the garden rustle as though it were raining.

It's eleven o'clock. As usual, I have only got to my desk at this late point. As always, I have to overcome an inhibition to get down to the text that has been 'resting' for almost two weeks—since we got back from Woserin. First I catch hold of one more news item—Interior Minister Schäuble has cancelled the funding for the cycling world championship in Stuttgart, because of the doping calamities in the sport. Then I make an appointment with the ear specialist, who'll probably have to prescribe me a hearing aid—not until mid-November. And then Annette calls as well—Hi, how are you?

She's not working until the afternoon today. No, it's not very nice on her own—Honza has a three-month residency in Wiepersdorf—she wasn't made to be on her own. Oh, the gloomy weather doesn't bother her, quite the opposite; she's always annoyed when the weather's nice outside and she has to sit inside. She asks for Tinka's number in Hamburg so she can wish her a happy birthday tomorrow. She has to go to Jena herself to hold a presentation and then she'll probably spend the weekend in Leipzig.

I allow myself one more distraction. Hanjo Kesting has sent a book that he brought out with Wallstein Verlag, *Begegnungen mit Hans Mayer. Aufsätze und Gespräche*. I flick through it, come across the phrase 'GDR literature' in one of the conversations, and Kesting's question: How large a role did the intellectuals and artists play in the political changes? Mayer refers to the French Revolution, for which the ground was laid mentally by the Enlightenment thinkers. 'I believe rather similar things happened in the GDR. Of course, the artists didn't "make" the events but they did have a role to play in them . . . And the rally on Alexanderplatz with writers such as Christa Wolf, Stefan Heym, Christoph Hein was a great moment . . . ' No comment.

I finally fetch my *City of Angels* text up onto the screen. Yesterday I read in old diaries that even then, 2004, I accused myself of procrastinating, laziness, fear of the manuscript. It almost consoles me— perhaps then it's not merely subjective inability, but a kind of inescapable law? I read the most recent section, the trip 'to the emigrants' houses' with Therese and Peter Gutman. Never took place in that form, not with these two but with Herr Schnauber, but I didn't want to introduce yet another character and I wanted to create an opportunity for conversations that were only possible with these two people—part of the ever-increasing exhilaration of inventing. Unscrupulously, I deviate, the longer the more, from the plain and naturalistic 'truth', as the protagonists will establish with disconcertment when they find themselves in the text. I'm looking for a connecting point for the chapter.

Telephone—Is that Wolf Hairdressers?

On the radio—sixteen nations discuss lowering greenhouse gas emissions at President Bush's invitation (Germany the seventh-worst polluter!). Bush prevents joint measures passed by the UN and counts on technical improvements and new nuclear power plants. 'A new era for humanity begins today!' He has considerably raised the budget for war expenditure for next year. A hopeless case—the Americans' realization that they can't continue their lives of luxury will come late, perhaps too late.

It is half past eleven. I am overcome by undeniable tiredness; how can anyone be so tired at this time of day? I slump down on my desk chair, fall asleep —perhaps for ten minutes. Awake with a start when Gerd comes in and asks, What's the loan word for spelling? Orthography! I stutter with sudden presence of mind. And Gerd, distrustful, Orthography? (My computer won't accept the alternative German spelling with an *f* instead of *ph*; it underlines it with an accusatory red squiggle.)

Gerd sets off on his daily shopping trip, which I envy him for, and I return to my text. There's a list of the episodes I still have to include, but I realize there's too much material that I have to breathe life into and organize and that I probably won't be able to include in full. I'll have the angel appear now and again—will it work? Will it stay that way?

Oh, radio. Major slash-and-burn land clearance in Brazil, producing a lot of CO_2. How much fruit and vegetables ought we to eat? Five portions a day, about 600 grams. I don't think I always manage that. Then they list all the illnesses that fruit and vegetables help or prevent; it's almost everything that puts us at risk.

Gerd brings up the post; a large parcel and mainly catalogues; there are more and more of them because they seem to sell addresses among themselves—*Börsenblatt*, Jokers, Eurotops, Torquato—flicking through these catalogues and putting bookmarks between the pages is one of my favourite pastimes. The second mass of post consists of invitations to exhibitions; it's incredible how many artists exhibit in how many galleries on how many days. Thirdly, there are almost always requests for donations, today for starving children in Africa, including a bank transfer form of course, which I fill in. As I'm doing so I think, if the damned governments around the world would only stop spending on armaments or at least cut spending by half, we could beat hunger.

A card from Nuria in Spain, an enticing photo of 'the delicacies that keep us here'. 'My soul takes the occasional downward slide,' she writes, 'but the Mediterranean light brightens even deep depths.' I know that she's sometimes depressed and that she tries to show it as little as possible, so her words are all the more surprising and unsettling. Another of the women I'd like to be closer to. Her birthday is on the same day as mine.

I flick through *Der Freitag*. An obituary for André Gorz. I read a detailed review of his slim, just-published book a few days ago—a letter to D., a love letter to his wife, with whom he lived for over fifty years. Neither of them could imagine ever surviving the other; she had been severely ill for years. Then, the day before yesterday, came the news that they had committed suicide together. That hit me hard. He, who thought radically and, as I believe, correctly, is described as timid and shy, having spoken very quietly. Another obituary suggests reading his books again now, which have apparently been unjustly forgotten; they harbour great foresight on the fate of the labour society and capitalism, says the article.

Gerd comes back heavily loaded from his shopping trip, as ever, having bought 'exotic spices'—seeds for sprinkling on salads, star anise, turmeric, chilli powder and a number of other little packets and tins. He homes in on lunch; the pasta in the fridge from last time is heated up to go with the vegetable ragout. It tastes good.

I flick through the new catalogues and at half past
two I lie down, relieved, and very tired as I always am
by this time. Read a little of Lizzie Doron's book.
Then I sleep. I wake up, as I sometimes do now, with
a scream. Listen to the rest of the book programme
in the kitchen—a collection of Jurek Becker's essays
has come out. I hear his voice and many an encounter
comes back to me. He was an upright person. I hear
on the radio that his father didn't speak to him for a
long time after the book *Jakob the Liar*. You can kid
the stupid Germans about the ghetto, he said. But not
me. I was there.

We have a cup of tea in the living room. Gerd has
brought home a piece of 'cold dog' cake, layers of bis-
cuits and chocolate in hardened coconut oil, which I
used to make for the children's birthdays. I remember
the taste but I only eat a tiny slice; it's very fatty.

Then I wrap the presents for Tinka's family,
whose birthdays are all in the next ten days. Tinka had
chosen her presents herself from a catalogue, Martin
is getting the obligatory sweater, Anton a book about
Tokyo, where he's sure to end up going as a Japanol-
ogist, and Helene a large African bag. Both children
are getting a small amount of cash too because they
need something to wear.

Then I go about the weekly measurement of my
INR value, always rather tense, but it's fine—2.6.
They told me I always have to take the blood thinner
Falithrom because of my pacemaker, so I always have

to measure my INR value—thrombosis prevention. Age demands its tribute.

Another task before I can get to the computer— I fill out the form to change from the electricity supplier Vattenfall to Lichtblick, who only produce electricity from regenerative sources—water, biomass, solar energy, wind power—without coal or nuclear power.

I make corrections on the last pages of *City of Angels* until six o'clock; I see the streets of Pacific Palisades that we drove up and down, the network that connected up the individual points—the emigrants' houses. A unique cluster of intellect and culture.

At seven o'clock, as most days, the first evening news on television. The liberation of the German engineer being held hostage in Afghanistan for weeks has failed; Burmese junta makes brutal attacks on demonstrators; at the donor conference in Berlin, a large sum of money has been released to fight dangerous infectious diseases in third world countries; run-up to Stoiber's exit in Bavaria; ex-minister Kanther has been given a lenient punishment for embezzlement—only a fine, which means he won't have a criminal record and continues to receive his full pension; a commission has found errors in many school textbooks, which is also to do with the deplorable federalist education system; Germany's women's football team plays Brazil on Sunday.

I watch the beginning of the early evening crime show and then Martin comes by to pick up the presents for his family; he and Anton are going to Hamburg tomorrow, Helene is coming by plane from Brussels and then they'll celebrate all four birthdays over the weekend. Tinka's new job in Hamburg means different focuses are forming in the family, but their very close connection is by no means weakened.

Martin says he's working on his convalescence after his rather unhappy job for the Hauptmann memorial site in Erkner; he's longing to get back to 'making art'. He has dinner with us; interrogations on family news. Martin went to a joint exhibition of various galleries in Wedding and says he can't usually relate to the exhibits. We flick through a catalogue announcing an art auction with a few big names. Carlfriedrich Claus is in there and Gerd talks again about his plan to raise his profile with a biography, but none of the publishers are interested. They calculate it won't sell very well. It would be just the right work to captivate Gerd for the next few years and it would suit him well. As it is, he may always be busy, sometimes even very much so, but he is lacking this one central task. That troubles me.

It's raining hard when Martin leaves, so he takes one of our waterproofs on his bicycle.

We watch part of an old crime show on television, which is being shown in honour of Jürgen Roland, who has died, and then switch over to ARTE where they're showing Antonioni's *Zabriskie Point*. It's the perfect conclusion and fits in with the day's main theme. I've seen the film before, in Los Angeles, but I can't recall where exactly and on what occasion. I can barely remember the film itself, either, but now I watch closely—the streets of Los Angeles, the campus where the students demonstrate, then the girl's long, long trip to the desert and the boy's daredevil flight. Their overlong lovemaking in the desert sand. The unforgettable image of all the couples suddenly lying around them—a vision. The inserts of normal consumers. The boy's futile, tragic death when he brings back the plane. And finally the girl's evil eye, exploding everything it stares at—the whole dead consumer civilization that destroys everything young and alive, and which can only be countered, or so the film tells us, with counter-destruction.

I think Antonioni's diagnosis was right. The state of affairs is even worse today, because our dead culture is under attack from a perhaps 'more barbaric', at least more alive culture—Islamism. In fact, the more vital attackers have always won such battles over history, and the tired apocalyptic culture has been defeated. Should things go differently this time? Because we—at this point—have the more horrific weapons? I really don't know. My image of the future is not a friendly one.

All this goes through my mind as I lie in bed. It is after midnight by now. This day too has passed.

Saturday, 27 September 2008

would have been the 'day of the year'. It was a Saturday on which I was at home for an interim stay between two periods in hospital; my wound was regarded as 'almost closed' but my knee got more and more swollen, despite lymph drainage. It started to scare me and I wrote the first line above, no more. In the afternoon Jana and Frank came by with little Nora and I held her for the first time, the great joy in this otherwise joyless summer, in which I spent almost all the time in hospitals since the knee joint operation on 11 June, up to 18 November; that's five months—they call it 'disturbed wound healing', and it afflicts approx. 1 per cent of patients . . .

I am writing this on 13 December. I don't want to dismiss the day altogether; I want to try to write something in retrospect about how I've been 'situated' in the past six months. It won't be easy. The time in hospital seems like an uneventful, unstructured period; I can barely distinguish the various rooms in the various hospitals in my memory. I was in the Immanuel Hospital, in the Charité (the 'bed tower'!), three days in the Hoppegarten convalescence clinic, in the Virchow Clinic, in the Protestant Geriatric Medical Centre. Six (or seven?) operations, all under general anaesthetic, to which I developed an aversion and something akin to fear—because I knew and had heard that many people, especially older patients, are confused after an anaesthetic and stay that way in some cases (students came over the subsequent days to interrogate me—my name, where we were, telephone number, date, ward, etc.—all of which I was able to answer without hesitation).

Whenever I think back I see myself lying on a stretcher being pushed along corridors by porters to the respective operation room, which I can barely tell apart, however. Only that all these subterranean, cold, grey, artificially lit rooms seemed like unfavourable workplaces for the operators and their teams. They themselves appeared not to think so, and the cold hardly troubled them—they said they experienced an adrenaline rush at every operation. The various recovery rooms. On one occasion I was very cold. Slight nausea. After that, usually a total lack of appetite so I managed to lose weight. Gerd brings me soups.

I'm fetching up details from the unstructured time, which incidentally appears to me as a bright, overexposed period. I can barely summon a memory of the separate nurses—although they were each important to me and did take on individuality. I observed how one becomes dependent on them as a patient and how one loses one's sense of shame, to a certain degree.

The interest in outside events wanes as well. What is now called the 'financial crisis' occurred during my time in hospital—essentially, the collapse of the capitalist world order—and the terrorist attacks in Bombay, India; I registered everything precisely, read the newspaper every day, was amazed and very much understood the significance of these events, yet I could not relate them to myself. If I had to put that feeling into words, I'd probably say—none of it affects me any more. My time is up. I watch events unfolding. At eighty, one is no longer part of it. This is no longer my time.

In other words—this summer of sickness has given me a good hard shove into old age. I fear one's eightieth birthday is the border between old age and closeness to death. In the corridors, I came across other patients, on crutches like me, who seemed even older and more helpless, until I called myself to order and said to myself, they're just as old as I am, I just don't want to see it.

I didn't think of work at all, although my *City of Angels* manuscript is piling up before me like an insurmountable peak. I didn't write a single line—not even a card to anyone. The doctor said my brain was occupied with processing the anaesthetics. Annette says I switched to 'autopilot'.

A lot of things left me cold. The only thing that interested me was everything to do with my family. I became aware that this is the fixed, permanent element of my life—only after the family comes everything connected to my work. Besides that, I occasionally dipped into one of my books, which I had asked to be brought in so I could give them to people—*Leibhaftig, Der Worte Adernetz, Christa T.* I read the texts as if for the first time, couldn't remember having written them, and to my amazement I found them 'not bad'. Actually, I thought, I've said everything I had to say. Couldn't I regard my '*oeuvre*' as complete? Must I still get down to the heavy labour on *City of Angels*? The question is unanswered to this day.

I read a great deal; *Magic Mountain* and the newcomer Uwe Tellkamp with *The Tower*, which I thought overrated. I watched television every night until almost midnight. I had the distinct feeling that I was letting time pass idly and that that was a misdemeanour. Partly, this 'laziness' or lethargy had broken out some time before my stay in hospital, and it is still on-going now, so it is of a more essential nature—an inhibition against 'writing', composed of the realization of the futility of this activity and of doubts in my own ability to master this new challenge at this point in my life.

On one occasion, my ward doctor, whom I had given a copy of *Leibhaftig*, asked whether I stood by my statement on 'futility' that I explained on one page of the book. Yes, I stand by it—once one has realized it, the real point is to carry on regardless, in the knowledge that the meaning of life is life, which one ought to lead with strength and dedication, even though it is not granted permanency . . .

Once, after around two thirds of the time, something remarkable happened. I heard (in my mind?) a voice that said clearly, Now you're going to get well. It was at midnight. I believed the voice straight away and I called Tinka, thinking she was most likely to be awake still. She wasn't, though. I left a message on her answering machine. The next morning she called, very agitated, to ask what I'd wanted in the middle of the night. I didn't remember my call to begin with, and then it came back to me. Perhaps that was when my recovery set in.

I got wind of the diverse reflexes of G.'s birthday —he turned eighty, and I couldn't be there. And he was incredibly active, had to organize his own celebration, essentially; I was scared he'd collapse one day. But he survived it all. Perhaps all the activity was his way of dealing with the sensitive date.

There was also the terrible wave of terror in Bombay and the explosion of the incredible international ('global') financial crisis. Another watershed; this time it is capitalism that has to swear its oath of disclosure. I think big business and politicians are in a state of utter dismay, which they are still seeking to conceal from the common consumers. And the common people refuse to acknowledge the change and try to go on as before—in other words, plenty of Christmas shopping, as though nothing had happened.

All this I acknowledged conscientiously, but it only affected me peripherally; in fact I became aware that I no longer know the kind of inner participation I once felt in conflicts, simply because the present (political) situation no longer plunges me into conflicts—I no longer feel responsible for what happens.

I wanted no influences from outside—no visitors, no phone calls if possible, wrote not a single line to anybody. (Now I hear I was a 'changed person'.)

I was afraid of the repeated operations—especially the anaesthetics. I survived them without the not-uncommon interim stage of confusion but I seem to have needed a lot of energy to process the consequences. When I came down with pneumonia on top of it all, the diagnosis apparently horrified and terrified my family—I was less upset; strangely enough I didn't have the feeling I might die of it, instead lay rigged up rather without emotion to the many machines in the intensive-care ward and admired the nurses for their competence.

Then later, back in the 'normal ward' and the geriatric ward under Dr Steinhagen-Thiessen, when they wanted to 'mobilize' me—that is, got me out of bed, forced me to take physiotherapeutic exercise—I fought this compulsion with mental resistance and was angry at the physiotherapists; I wanted nothing but to stay in bed in peace and was glad when the sessions were cancelled. This lethargy has stayed with me; I still do too little exercise to strengthen the muscles in my right leg. (I'm familiar with it from the time after my hip operations.)

All in all, this time—the whole summer—seemed 'shallower', no doubt because my emotions displayed no upward or downward peaks. I think this state is due to my age, not necessarily related to my illness. I dreamt a lot and in great detail—and have forgotten everything. When reading, I had to make sure the books weren't too exciting. I was terribly sensitive so most crime novels were out of the question. I read Thomas Mann's *Magic Mountain* and (cursorily) Uwe Tellkamp's *The Tower*—an overrated book about a Dresden milieu before 1989. Watched television until midnight every night.

I was aware that this time was a caesura. I was (and am) often not in a very good mental state. The thought of death is omnipresent. And the awareness that the years are now heading towards it. The drive for new work is minor, above all the question— what for?

Sunday, 27 September 2009

Woserin

In the first half hour after midnight, I go on reading
the book published by Faber und Faber, *Wie viele Leben
lebt der Mensch* by Walter Markov ('a posthumous
autobiography'). Markov was a historian and social
scientist and taught at Leipzig when I was a student
there, and was one of the critical Marxists along with
Ernst Bloch, Hans Mayer and Robert Schulz. I'd
expected to find a description of the conflicts at our
faculty, which barely affected me at the time. But to
my disappointment, the book is rather loosely written
and hardly refers to the serious problems; for example, why he, Markov, was expelled from the party in
the early fifties and what exactly the consequences
were for him. All this is dealt with quite superficially;
did the writer still want to refrain from criticizing the
party when he wrote that particular passage? Instead,
he describes in great detail how he met his wife and
the births of their (five) children, along with the personnel policy at the university with a wealth of names
that say nothing to me now.

I couldn't get to sleep and then, reluctantly, took half a Stilnox at around one. (They're addictive! say the doctors, but what's going to happen if you get a bit addicted at the age of eighty?) There's probably a dash of autosuggestion in it if I can really sleep after this half a tablet. Then, like today, I wake at seven and fight to fall asleep again, which usually falls flat. Then the one or two hours until I get up are torturous, close to depression, occupied by oppressive thoughts —death, every day death—against which even listing all the positive things of which my life actually consists has little effect. I try out mantras to help me fall asleep but they don't work. Hours I am afraid of.

I get up shortly before nine, as always with terrible lower back pain that only lets off a little after some movement but still usually hinders me from walking without pain. Gerd already in the kitchen, fully dressed. Shower and wash my hair while listening to a programme on Deutschlandradio Kultur, *Allein gegen alle*, a repeat of an ancient broadcast but still good fun.

News. Some sixty million German citizens can vote for their new parliament today, then. We voted by postal ballot for Wolfgang Thierse (SPD) as our individual candidate and gave our party vote to Die Linke—hesitantly of course, but the SPD has been too mushy and incapable of making approaches to Die Linke, which would be the only possibility to form a bloc 'left of centre'. So they need a strong left-wing opposition.

Iris Berben is interviewed on the radio. She's starring in a new sixty-eight film (*Es kommt der Tag*), as a woman who was an activist in 1968, gave away her child, changed her identity and is now confronted by her adult child turning up again. (West Germany's trauma, in which we have no part, as they have no part in our traumas—even this prevents the much-lauded 'growing together'.)

News. Iran has launched two new short-range rockets; in the Philippines, a terrible tropical storm is causing massive floods. Dead and injured, many people homeless.

Breakfast. Bread and sausage. Medications because the cough that's been plaguing me for a week refuses to go away—Gelomyrtol, Locabiosol spray.

On the radio (this is turning into a media day!) they recall the Congress for Cultural Freedom that took place in Berlin in 1950, an anti-communist event from which the journal *Der Monat* emerged, among other things. All of it, as we now know, financed by the CIA. At the beginning comes the voice of Arthur Koestler, remembering the words of the New Testament—But let your communication be, Yea, yea; Nay, nay: for whatsoever is more than these cometh of evil.

Annette calls. She and Honza went to Weimar for an event that I was originally supposed to go to as well, with the title 'Freedom That I Mean'. Very well organized, very many writers for discussions and readings, over two days, but very few people in the audience. Disappointing. Annette still hasn't quite got rid of her infection either, which always gets trapped in her sinuses, but she's on leave next week so she can make a full recovery. She has to work too much. Gerd advises her to go on a three-month trip to Italy. She can't do that, what with Honza's blood-cleansing appointments, but she'd like to give it a try for a month. I tell her about the fairly long telephone conversation with Benni, who is now two weeks into his carpentry apprenticeship and is enjoying it. We're very glad of it.

Honza went to visit his publishing house in Cologne. The editor is very enthusiastic about his book; they've already designed the cover and it's coming out in spring.

I call Hamburg and Martin picks up the telephone. The weather's wonderful and they're showing the Seidels around Hamburg, bought vegetables at the fish market for Tinka's birthday tomorrow; they're expecting eighteen guests. They seem to be becoming enthusiastic Hamburg residents.

Gerd comes. He's busy with my manuscript, which will cost me a good few corrections. He is bothered by my formulation, 'The new faith comes cunningly via the mind.' And the old one? he asks. Did it not come via the mind too? Or where else did it come from? Via emotions, I say. And if it came via the mind then it was a different part of the mind. Gerd is sceptical about the whole Lily plot—is it necessary? What's the point of the philosopher? He still thinks I mean Walter Benjamin, but that's not the case (any more)! It would be a lot of work if I had to make changes, and I'm afraid of that. Gerd says we ought to show the manuscript to someone impartial who's not familiar with the events it's based on. I agree.

As I'm taking strong fluid retention tablets on Dr Etzold's orders, originally to dissolve a blockage in my lung, I am constantly having to dash to the toilet.

Gerd chops the meat for the pea soup and gives me the rib bones, which I like to chew on.

It's after twelve and we go out. I on my two sticks as always, which I haven't been able to go without since my knee operation in June of last year. It depresses me a great deal—although it's certainly partly my own fault; not enough exercise and not hard enough. Today I wonder whether I simply ought to get used to the state of affairs. Others have to as well.

A marvellous day. Incredibly intense colours. A sky in an unreal shade of blue. The trees are still green; isolated leaves, yellowed, are falling. The horse chestnuts, however, have been gnawed bare by the leaf miners, their leaves brown on the ground. They're supposed to be buried—but who bothers?

Aside from that, it hasn't rained for three weeks; everything is barren and dry, the grass greyish brown and the sheep have trouble finding a few blades. Is it to do with climate change, which the latest studies say is coming even faster than previously assumed?

I walk down the bumpy grass to the road; that's far too little, of course, but there is hardly any smooth stretch I could walk on nearby. Apart from that, I'm lazy.

I sit down on a garden chair in the sun and read the *Schweriner Volkszeitung*, which ends up with us because Andrea's not here at the moment. On the first page, thirty passport photos of people saying why they're going to vote. Among them Hermann Kant, who doesn't expect much of the new government but wants to make use of his right to vote nonetheless. Iran building second uranium plant; an article about the psychology of shopping—we spend money either to buy something or to experience something; 'Be happy, Erik'—a thirteen-year-old from Kritzkow wants to become Germany's most courageous school student; there are 1.4 million people entitled to vote in Mecklenburg Western Pomerania, with 80,000 voting for the first time; Merkel and Steinbrück at G20 summit; more work, less pay— what can be done? Shipbuilders to waive pay; readers' letters: the Russians' invasion of East Poland had a history; shot in the face—situation escalates at police station after domestic argument.

Pea soup for lunch, a favourite childhood dish.

We lie down and confirm to each other how tired we always are in the middle of the day. I sleep—with a break to read—until four o'clock.

Then no more peace to work on this text. Tea and a biscuit in the television room. I read the culture supplement of *Der Spiegel* with book recommendations, none of which I find very enticing, certainly not once I've read extracts, which I usually find banal.

The first election predictions at six, then, and our worst fears come true—the new government under Angela Merkel will be a Christian Democrat–Liberal coalition. Westerwelle from the FDP probably foreign minister. The worst election result for the SPD since 1949. CDU 33.4. SPD 22.7. FDP 14.8. Die Linke 12.5. Greens 10.6.

The Pirate Party, which our grandsons supported, got 2 per cent.

Then of course the usual celebratory orgies by the winners, from the losers the promise to analyse the lousy results, interviews with voters and party people, including the leaders. No one will indulge in speculation over personnel changes yet.

Platzeck is the winner again in Brandenburg, the SPD hasn't lost and Die Linke is the second-strongest party, well before the CDU.

That puts an end to our evening.

Annette calls—Well, what do you say? Rotten, huh? She'd said she could never vote for Die Linke because of the old cadre who were still in the party, but she forgives us for it—what with 'our past'.

We'd planned to drink a margarita—no matter how the election turned out. We do so now, with anchovy and shrimp canapés.

Tinka calls. Shit on a stick, she says. We say what there is to say. For my cough, she passes on a prescription from Seidel, who's a doctor—five cups of sage tea a day, with honey.

We watch a crime show we've seen before (*Der doppelte Lott*). I fall asleep in the middle and then I manage to watch the talk show with Anne Will afterwards while Gerd goes to bed, not forgetting to take off my surgical stocking for me first. He's having to develop more and more carer's skills—to my sorrow.

The old pros from each party have come together for the discussion, and present sensible arguments— Baum from the FDP, Frau Süßmuth from the CDU, Egon Bahr from the SPD. He says the SPD must and will renew itself, and yes, it will remain a major party for the people, as it has something to offer for all classes of society. Now it has to make ready for a battle for justice. He's astoundingly fit for a man of eighty-seven. No, he says, there can be no approaching Die Linke as long as they don't stand by the basic law on foreign policy, demanding that Germany leaves NATO and the like. How he wants to achieve a 'left-wing bloc' left of centre on this basis, I don't know.

Off to bed, just before twelve. While undressing, I once again notice a phenomenon I only became aware of a few weeks ago, when I read in Oliver Sacks that a number of people are affected by musical hallucinations. That is, they constantly hear music, more or less loudly and absolutely involuntarily.

It can become a real nuisance. And it occurred to me that when I listen in to my mind, I actually always catch myself with a song, sung very quietly inside me. Often, in the car or when I'm sitting outside, I hum it to myself; Tinka has pointed it out before. (Now, for example, I catch myself singing the tune to the verse, 'Ich möcht' am liebsten sterben, da wär's auf einmal still'.) To my amazement, they are often hymns singing inside me. This time, when I listen, 'So nimm denn meine Hände . . . ' I don't usually notice it, and thankfully it doesn't bother me because it's very quiet. But now I've been prompted to pay attention to it.

I read for a little while, a very extensive Robert Oppenheimer biography by Kai Bird and Martin J. Sherwin, who bring out very strongly how during the early fifties in the USA, Oppenheimer, the 'father of the atomic bomb', came under ineffable fire from the Republicans because of his alleged communist past when he wanted to restrict the deployment of this weapon, horrified by the consequences of his creation, and what humiliating interrogations he was subjected to, which repressive measures were taken against him and how he was afterwards a 'broken man'. As always in such cases, I am overcome by depression and despondence—nothing can be done against this kind of malice and stupidity.

In the middle of the night I take a valerian tablet, read the very well done catalogue about the construction of the Berlin Palace—not exactly my favourite architectural project—and then actually manage to go back to sleep with no stronger sleeping tablets.

I have an incredibly long dream that takes place in a luxury hotel and presents a veritably novelistic plot—with a huge meal, exclusion of one (my) person, with intrigues and injuries, collapses and meetings with old acquaintances including writers, but I don't know them. It seems to me I've never had a dream like this. When I wake up I tell myself as much as possible of the twisted plots, though they do gradually fade.

I don't get up until after nine.

Monday, 27 September 2010

Berlin

Midnight was the end of Denis Scheck's book programme *Druckfrisch* on television. He looked at the title *Deutschland schafft sich ab* by Thilo Sarrazin, who has been hounded through the media and political events in an inconceivable way in the past two weeks and yet still almost made it straight to the top of the bestseller list from nowhere. Scheck was indignant that the chancellor had dismissed the book before even reading it, that the president (Wulff) practically ordered the federal bank, Sarrazin's employer, to fire him, only to then hastily agree to his dismissal. We didn't find out whether Scheck himself rejects the book or accepts it for its allegedly accurate description of conditions among asylum seekers, and criticizes it—like almost everyone—for the claim that asylum seekers are not capable of being educated for genetic reasons. At any rate, a large part of the population seems to be of the opinion that the immigrants, particularly the Muslims, are only out to fleece us and ought to be given harsher treatment.

Glad to get to bed, as always. Lying down is one of the most delightful moments of the day. I'm always very tired and keep falling asleep, for example, in the evenings, even during my crime shows . . .

At the moment I'm reading Markus Wolf's autobiography, with much sympathy at times. Much of it is simply objectively interesting, for instance, Herbert Wehner's strange toing and froing, which can only be explained by assuming that Wehner, at his core perhaps not yet quite dis-attached from communism, sensed a renewed danger of war in the West's postwar policy, which had to be dealt with by informing the East. Another interesting aspect—that Otto John really was kidnapped, not by the Stasi but by the KGB, with whom his friend, a doctor with whom he spent the evening, was collaborating.

Last night I read the sections about the building of the Wall, which wasn't Ulbricht's idea but an order from Khrushchev, who was afraid the mass flight from the GDR would cause the state to collapse, making his western flank vulnerable. And the leaders of the Western world were apparently relieved that a weak point in Europe's peace and security was eliminated by the GDR securing its borders. Wolf and his 'service' were just as surprised by the Wall as we all were, and he describes the general public's reaction very realistically. Just as all in all—if one accepts the premise that these 'services' were simply necessary and that he saw his task specifically as contributing to peace—just as he is then rather 'decent' all in all.

Nevertheless, I feel constantly divided as I read—he claims to have had nothing to do with the Stasi on the domestic front and their sordid actions, and he was in a constant clinch with Mielke, and yet—can he really cut himself off from it? Does he not have his own skeletons in the closet, for example, those of the 'burnt' spies whose covers were blown?

As always, I take a Vivinox at bedtime; I'm probably too used to them now. But since I read what a mixture Thomas Mann used to force down his throat every night . . . Of course, as I'm falling asleep the images pass by my mind's eye that I saw in the years Wolf describes. The fact that we were also relieved, because we too saw how the GDR was leeching, and we wanted it to stay alive, and we hoped too that another spirit would now move in. Why couldn't we see at the time that this 'spirit' did not exist in the apparatus as it was—never could exist?

Turning out the light is always a moment of relief. Another day over without a personal catastrophe. We're still alive. We're alive. I always resolve to accept every day, every hour of this life without reservation, and always the thought of death underpins almost every hour. And the knowledge of how short the period of time is becoming that remains to me, to us. The horrific idea of having to live alone. Many times a day, I look at Gerd, what he's doing, his facial expression, his posture, how he says something. The way he brings in a surprising dish for dinner, sometimes triumphant. I listen for the sound of his breathing. I can't very well wake him to tell him how much I love him.

Then, like every evening, I go through the children and grandchildren. No particular reason for concern, I think, not even with Tinka and Martin any more. Honza is under constant stress with his book, readings and events. Benjamin seems to be sticking to his carpentry apprenticeship; that would be admirable. Helene is happy with her Till and, as she said recently, has 'got the worst over with', namely, a double workload in her job for several weeks. Anton announced on the telephone that he'd be coming to the Thomas Mann Prize ceremony with 'someone else'. That 'someone else' is his 'dearest' by the name of Lea. A new trait in him, simply saying it like that. I'm glad. And Jana and Frank were literally floating in happiness at their wedding and are now on their honeymoon in Istanbul. That leaves little Nora, whom I think of so often although I see her so rarely. A wonderful child, a miracle like every child. Annette, the exuberant grandmother, keeps me up to date on her progress, particularly in learning to speak at the moment.

I repeat my mantra—I'm doing fine. I'm doing fine.

I fall asleep and sleep almost through the night, without dreams, which are otherwise usually very lively and very strange.

In the morning I read some more of Markus Wolf's book—it's called *Spionagechef im geheimen Krieg*, incidentally, and was first published in English by Random House in 1997 with the title *Man without a Face*, interestingly enough; it is hardly known here. As always, I put off getting up. Gerd is reading Claude Lanzmann's autobiography and thinks he makes too much of himself—goodness, what a Superman! Then he's the first to use the bathroom, as he almost always is. Sitting on the edge of the bed, I look out of the window. Amalienpark is still entirely green. When you look high up at the tops of the trees, though, you can see they're turning very yellow.

The usual morning toilette, shower and so on. For several weeks, a breathing spray has been part of the routine, because a lung doctor voiced the suspicion that I might be developing slight asthma. I am short of breath, I must admit, sometimes more, sometimes less. Getting dressed, I need three creams and ointments: one for my back (I don't really believe it works), one for the hard skin that has recently been forming on my left big toe, one for the scar on my knee, which shows no further reaction to all the ointments, however. Sometimes I think my body has left me in the lurch, and I don't like being in company for that reason.

Breakfast—a slice of bread, ham, tea, an apple, peeled and prepared by Gerd. The *Berliner Zeitung*. On the front page, beneath the headline 'Berlin, Schönefelder Kreuz', is a photo of a Polish tour bus that crashed into a bridge pier yesterday, killing thirteen. The passengers were coming back from holiday in Spain. Then—coalition provokes unemployed; only

five euro more for adult benefits recipients. The
government swears that it made its measurements
based on the lowest income level, as ordered by the
constitutional court, which still ought to be slightly
higher than long-term unemployment benefit. The
real scandal is that there's no minimum level for low
incomes, so they can be kept so outrageously low—
and then they're used to calculate the even lower
income, unemployment benefit! The measurement
basis for the calculations is presented on the second
page. Third page—Tacheles, the alternative art project
on Oranienburgerstraße, is under threat. Below that,
'Simply Living in Freedom'—memorial service at the
Academy of Arts for Bärbel Bohley, who has died of
cancer. The article recalls her statement, 'We wanted
justice and got a constitutional state.' I'm very sorry
about her premature death. Page 4—op-ed by Arno
Widmann, discrimination is necessary. On the new
long-term unemployment benefit calculations. In
essence—those who haven't paid into the system have
no right to receive payments back from it. They ought
to be helped. But they must also understand that they
are supplicants, that they need help. Column—'The
Angry Wealthy' by Paul Krugman. How America's
rich are fighting Obama for their privileges. (Sadly,
Obama will probably not hold out against this
embittered resistance.) Page 6—SPD special party
conference. Gabriel trying to build party's profile
(but do they have a candidate for the chancellor in
2012?). Stasi's secret knowledge used. West German

intelligence service took over GDR cipher experts (Stasi everywhere at the moment, on the twentieth anniversary of unification).

Business—bankers earning big bucks again (one can hardly credit the cheek after the crisis!); IMF sees robust growth in Germany; trade unions warn of significant increase in contract work; uninhabitable for decades—Greenpeace has calculated the consequences of a nuclear disaster for the Krümmel and Biblis B power stations. (The coalition wants to extend the operating lives of the nuclear power stations without having found a solution for storing nuclear waste.) The article describes how the risk of an accident like Chernobyl in German nuclear power stations is not equal to zero, and above all they are insufficiently protected against accidents or attacks from the air. A nightmare they are forcing us to live with—for reasons of costs! More and more people going online via mobile devices—and we don't even have a cell phone! As usual, I don't bother with the sports pages.

Arts section—strangely enough, the headline 'Christa T. Now Works in Accounts'. A photographer and the editor Arno Widmann are travelling around the republic until 2 October in search of unity. Widmann names a young woman from the GDR, who has become a tax clerk, 'Christa T.' of all names. Is this a new attempt at rapprochement after his terribly unfortunate review of *City of Angels* (which he insisted was a 'declaration of love')? His articles are usually interesting and intelligent, but the man is a mystery to me. Below the line—post-mortem; new funeral possibilities, burying ashes beneath a tree in a forest casket made of pressed maize and potato starch, and so on. The cemeteries are no longer large enough. And it seems that many relatives no longer want to have to visit a grave. I spare myself the reviews of theatre performances I'll never see, as we don't go out in the evenings at all any more, sadly— because I'm so hampered by my crutches. One thing only—Uwe Tellkamp's *The Tower* has been adapted and staged in Dresden; 600,000 copies of his novel have now been sold.

Berlin—deadly end to a works outing. Photos and closer description of the bus accident near Schönefeld, in which thirteen Polish passengers died. Page 2— protest against the new flight routes above southwest Berlin after construction of the new airport in Schönefeld. Page 3—only the spectators are cold. All-day rain at the thirty-seventh Berlin marathon. Page 4—young people and education: school pupils' university at the FU on climate and energy; save the loops and hitches—handwriting must be retained!; Shell youth study: full of concern and confidence. Page 5—arrived but not accepted—the strictly religious Islamic Federation celebrates its thirtieth anniversary and argues over integration. Also— Tuscany in Brandenburg. And—Peter and the Wolfgang Thierse; Thierse has recorded a CD of *Peter and the Wolf* and is donating the income to charity.

A deliberately detailed listing of the newspaper stories so as to make a record of what's officially occupying us. Unofficially, we are expecting the Spanish ambassador and Gerd is searching the shelves ('a terrible mess!') for Spanish translations of my books; he doesn't find much, most of it in Catalan. Hands me a book, *sich aussetzen—das Wort ergreifen*, that was made for me for my eightieth birthday and also contains an article from the Catalan Marta Pessarrodona, which I'd forgotten, like most of what's in the book. Now I flick through it; Marta says that she's always integrated me into Berlin's biography and that she came to our flat on Friedrichstraße in 1984. I have no memory of it. Nor of her being there again in 1987 and reading *Accident*. But then she writes about our visit to Barcelona, how she accompanied us to the spot from where you can see Gaudí's Sagrada Família. And we have Nuria Quevedo's beautiful picture of that view on our wall.

Gerd gives me a few items of post taken in by the Schweizers while we were away—a book from Gerhard Begrich (from Erfurt), Radius Verlag, *Schönheit gilt es zu schauen*, with the subtitle *Theologie und Poesie*. Alongside a sincere dedication, it contains an essay about me, 'Was bleibt. Nachdenken über Christa Wolf'. The authors' considerations from a Christian perspective on various of my texts, in the sense that these texts had always helped them and given them hope.

Then a quite long, intense letter from a woman from Berlin, prompted by *City of Angels*, which she calls a 'captivating and liberating' text. My books, she writes, have accompanied her for more than half her life (people often tell me that now). She goes on to thank me for staying 'in this part of the country', and talks about 1989 as a 'brief period of trying out utopia'. I could cite more of this letter, which is typical of a large number of letters I've received since *City of Angels*. More from the East—but not only from there—more women than men, more older than very young people. Testaments of personal concern, which push aside my doubts over whether I ought to have published the book in this form.

The reader has sent me a book by Peter Handke, *Versuch über den geglückten Tag. Ein Wintertagtraum*, which I don't know yet. I read the motto, 'Winter's day—on the horse, the shadow freezes'. I like that sentence a great deal.

Honza calls to ask how to stress the word 'jury'. He has another reading tonight and is busy as a bee; his book is on the shortlist for the book prize in Frankfurt. He's exhausted; all this advance waiting time is very hard for him. I think it shouldn't be done to writers. I do wish for him and Annette that he gets the prize though.

The expected Spanish ambassador comes at twelve—an almost inconspicuous, polite, modest man, not too full of himself and apparently not merely pretending an interest. He wants to meet me before I receive the honorary doctorate from the University of Madrid at the embassy on the 4th of October. We drink good sherry that Gerd bought especially for the occasion. He asks how we feel now, on the twentieth anniversary of reunification, and I attempt to give a balanced answer—but what form can that take now? Should one argue against the facts as they are now? Should one warm up the old deficits? The ambassador says people abroad see reunification as a success story, and talks about the difficulties they're having in Spain—the crisis has hit them very hard, 20 per cent unemployment (while here the labour market is allegedly 'booming'—albeit very many temporary workers, short-time workers, etc.). The Spanish are more optimistic than the Germans, though, he says. He likes living in Berlin very much, finds it an interesting, lively city (I think so too, except that I almost only look at that liveliness from inside).

We exchange books and the ambassador says goodbye. We eat stir-fried vegetables and rice, then lie down; that's at coming up for two o'clock. I read more of Markus Wolf's memoir. He offers proof that secret services are the 'world's second-oldest trade' from the Bible. Writes about specific cases, not without sympathy, including cases of defectors. I've had about enough of it and I sleep; always very tired in the middle of the day.

After four—we usually stay in bed that long—tea and a sliver of cherry cake. Instead of going back to this text I stay in front of the television—that happens all too often. (Sometimes I think, what couldn't I have done in all the countless hours I've spent in front of the TV!) I feel fine about it though; I have the feeling that the day is ebbing away and my bad mood or depression brightens slightly. I'm no longer so keen on being restlessly active all day long. The number of years I've lived often come into my mind, as an excuse, and what my daughters say when I complain that I'm lazy—you can really afford it now to be not as active at last. Well then.

So we zap between the channels during the afternoon schedules until *Soko 5113* comes on at last and then, on the other channel, *Großstadtrevier*. One knows the characters but I couldn't name a single one of the many cases I've watched. It's shameful.

We eat—salad, prawns, cheese. Gerd always tries to serve something in the evening that isn't 'just bread'.

Then we also watch the 'TV thriller' *Ein geheimnisvoller Sommer*, a constructed story starring Suzanne von Borsody, who makes the same upset face all the way through.

There are discussions on all channels about the coalition's decision to raise unemployment benefit by only five euros. They usually ignore the real problems and get stuck on this one figure.

Later, a man on a political magazine show reports on how he and his family were harassed and practically destroyed by the Stasi—with the twentieth anniversary of unification approaching, the Stasi are a big deal. A comment on the book by Markus Wolf, which I read for the final time this evening. As so often, I have to free myself consciously from hopeless thoughts for the big picture. I think about how to put this (but what?) into a piece of writing. I can't think of anything. I wouldn't be inconsolable if I didn't write any more.

27 September 2011

Headline *Berl. Ztg.*—Wowereit votes green. Coalition has only one-vote majority in Berlin city parliament.

Wake from a dream at three in the morning—before me lie three dead bodies, all foreigners, one of them is me, unrecognizable. Have the feeling I've been shot in the temples. Ties in with something I heard or read previously. Have to get used to being alone in the bedroom every time; the second bed is missing.

I read a few pages of the book about [Estela Canto's] relationship to Borges, which Ellen sent me. Didn't know B. was infertile—for mental reasons, not least due to his domineering mother.

Find the right position for sleeping; that takes time and strategy since I've been out of hospital. There's one position in which I'm not in pain. Decide not to go to the toilet chair yet, which I then have to do an hour later, shortly before 5—a sensitive operation. Take the 2nd half Stilnox tablet. Manage to sleep until almost 8.

This life between bed and chair now over 2 weeks . . . In-between terrible pain, which is now doped slightly using stronger pain patches. Great doubts about how it is to go on.

2nd half of the night. Read a few pages several times. Slept in between, to my surprise until shortly before 8 the last time.

Then read; I look for something to read that doesn't weigh me down too much—easily done. As always, a certain fear of the pain when I get up. Frau [. . .], who annoyed me to begin with, whom I've got used to more now. She is very zealous.

Toilet, washing, dressing in the bathroom. One even gets used to this child's status, albeit with difficulty. But—the other person is a nurse . . .

Breakfast. Egg on bread. Since they increased the pain patches, my appetite seems to be waning again. Ate a very few peas.

BZ—'It's going to be noisy over the Müggelsee'

Facsimiles of Handwritten Pages

27 September 2008

5)

6)

27 September 2011

Notes

These notes cover persons and contexts necessary to understand the diary entries. Names of public figures and events not directly related to the diary, with which readers can be assumed to be familiar, have not been included.

Members of the family mentioned in the text, alongside Christa Wolf (born Ihlenfeld, 1929; died Berlin, 2011) and Gerhard (Gerd) Wolf (born 1928):

Annette (born 1952), daughter of Christa and Gerhard Wolf; first marriage to the film director Rainer Simon (born 1941); second marriage to the Czech writer Jan (Honza) Faktor (born 1951).

Jana Simon (born 1972), Annette's daughter from her first marriage; her husband Frank Rothe (born 1972) and their daughter Nora (born 2008).

Benjamin Faktor (Benni, 1979–2012), Annette's son from her second marriage.

Katrin (Tinka, born 1956), daughter of Christa and Gerhard Wolf, and her husband Martin Hoffmann (born 1948), painter and graphic artist.

Helene Wolf (born 1982), Katrin and Martin's daughter.

Anton Wolf (born 1984), Katrin and Martin's son.

2001

City of God : E. L. Doctorow, *City of God* (New York: Random House, 2000). Quotes in this section are taken from pages 256, 116 and 190.

CDU: Christian Democratic Union of Germany, a centre-right, liberal-conservative political party whose leader, Angela Merkel, has been chancellor of Germany since 2005.

'Brecht's early lines . . .' : Bertolt Brecht, 'Of Poor B.B.' (Michael Hamburger trans.) in *Poetry and Prose* (Reinhold Grimm ed.) (New York: Continuum, 2003), p. 33.

'Association for the former Jewish orphanage': The Association of Supporters and Friends of the Former Jewish Orphanage in Pankow, founded in 2000, has the purpose of promoting the memory of former Jewish life and caring for sites of Jewish culture in Pankow. Christa Wolf was a member of the association's advisory committee until her death.

'The new book . . .' : Christa Wolf's short story 'Leibhaftig' was published by Luchterhand in 2002. The cover of the first edition was designed by Martin Hoffmann.

Adolf Dresen (1935–2001): Theatre and opera director; after staging productions at the Deutsches Theater in East Berlin, he went to West Germany in 1977; lived in Berlin after 1990; a friend of Christa and Gerhard Wolf.

Piece for an anthology: The text 'Assoziationen in Blau' [Associations in Blue] was published in the volume *Neruda Blau: Ein poetisches Spiel mit der 'schönsten aller Farben'* [Neruda Blue: A Poetic Game with the 'Most Beautiful of All Colours'] (Gabriele Pommerin-Götze ed.) (Gräfelfing: Realis, 2003). A year later, Nadine Gordimer included the piece in an English translation by Jan van Heurck in her anthology *Telling Tales* (London: Bloomsbury, 2004). Also in: Christa Wolf, *Mit anderem Blick. Erzählungen* [With Another View: Short Stories] (Frankfurt am Main: Suhrkamp Verlag, 2005), pp. 35–9.

Maria Sommer (born 1922): head of Gustav Kiepenheuer Bühnenvertriebs GmbH, honorary president of the authors' collecting society VG Wort; a close friend of Christa and Gerhard Wolf who represented their media rights.

The text that actually ought to be the centre of every day: Christa Wolf was working on the manuscript for *Stadt der Engel oder The Overcoat of Dr. Freud*, Berlin 2010. Translated by Damion Searls as *City of Angels; or, The Overcoat of Dr. Freud* (New York: Farrar, Straus and Giroux, 2012).

PDS: Party for Democratic Socialism, active between 1989 and 2007. It was the legal successor to the Socialist Unity Party of Germany (SED), which ruled the German Democratic Republic (East Germany) as a one-party state until 1990. The PDS was succeeded by the party Die Linke (The Left).

'A fairly long portrait of [Hans Stubbe]': 'Ein Besuch' [A Visit], written in 1968, published in the volume Christa Wolf, *Lesen und Schreiben* [Reading and Writing] (Berlin: Aufbau Verlag, 1971), for which Hans Stubbe wrote an afterword. Included in: Christa Wolf, *Werke* (Sonja Hilzinger ed.), *Volume 4: Essays/Gespräche/ Reden/Briefe, 1959–1974* (Munich: Luchterhand Literaturverlag, 1999), pp. 283–9.

'A new essay by Peter Hacks . . .': 'Zur Romantik'
[On Romanticism]. Published in book form as: *Zur
Romantik* (Berlin: Eulenspiegel Verlag, 2008).

Discussion circle: a monthly discussion circle run by
Christa Wolf, at which intellectuals from East and
West met from 1989 to 2005 to talk about current
political and cultural issues.

Peter Bender (1923–2008): German historian, writer and journalist; Berlin correspondent for WDR television; in the
1970s, ARD radio correspondent in Warsaw. He was a
proponent of Willy Brandt and Egon Bahr's *Ostpolitik*.

'What was it that Ingeborg Bachmann said . . .': Ingeborg
Bachmann, 'Die gestundete Zeit' [The Elapsed Time]
in *Die gestundete Zeit* (Munich: Piper Verlag, 1953).

2002

Red–green coalition: In European politics, an alliance of
'red' social-democratic parties with 'green' environ-
mentalist parties. In Germany, a red–green coalition
of the Social Democratic Party of Germany (SPD) and
Alliance '90 / The Greens, led by Chancellor Gerhard
Schröder, formed the federal government from
September 1998 to September 2005.

SPD: Social Democratic Party of Germany, one of the two
major contemporary political parties in Germany,
along with the Christian Democratic Union (CDU).

The Greens: Alliance '90/The Greens, often simply called
the Greens, formed in 1993 from the merger of the
German Green Party (founded in West Germany in
1980) and Alliance '90 (founded during the Revolution
of 1989–1990 in East Germany). The focus of the

party is on ecological, economic and social sustainability. From 1998 to 2005, the Greens were coalition partners in Chancellor Schröder's federal government.

PISA: The Programme for International Student Assessment gathers skills and knowledge of students worldwide and compares them internationally. It is a project of the Organisation for Economic Cooperation and Development (OECD).

The Tubachs: Frederic (Fritz) Tubach (born 1930), German studies professor at the University of California in Berkeley, and his wife Sally Patterson Tubach; friends of Christa and Gerhard Wolf.

OWEN: The Ost-West-Europäische FrauenNetzwerk (East–West European Women's Network) was founded in 1992 with the goal of encouraging cooperation between women active in civil society and politics, movements and organizations in Eastern and Western Europe. Katrin Wolf co-founded the network and worked there until 2003.

Ruth and Hans Misselwitz: Ruth Misselwitz (born 1952), Protestant pastor at the Alte Pfarrkirche in Pankow, co-founder of the Pankow Peace Circle. Hans Misselwitz (born 1950), member of the People's Chamber and parliamentary undersecretary of state in the foreign ministry of the last GDR government in 1990; from 1999 to 2005, office manager for Wolfgang Thierse in the SPD executive committee; from 2005 to 2010, managing director of the East German Forum for Social Democracy; from 2010, secretary of the SPD's values commission. Both friends of Christa and Gerhard Wolf.

Marina Beyer (born 1950): Behavioural biologist; member of the Pankow Peace Circle in the 1980s; equality officer for the last GDR government with Katrin Wolf as her personal assistant. Co-founder of OWEN.

Gerhard Rein (born 1936): Editor at Süddeutscher Rundfunk, reporting from the GDR from 1982; from 1992 to 1997, ARD radio correspondent for southern Africa. Recorded a highly significant interview with Christa Wolf on 8 October 1989, which was broadcast on almost all West German radio stations. See also Gerhard Rein's speech in *Wohin sind wir unterwegs? Zum Gedenken an Christa Wolf* [Where Are We Heading? In Memory of Christa Wolf] (Berlin: Suhrkamp Verlag, 2012), pp. 56–8).

2003

Ulrich Dietzel (born 1932): Long-standing head of the literature archive at the Academy of the Arts in East Berlin, academy director from 1990 to 1993. In 2003, he published *Männer und Masken. Kunst und Politik in Ostdeutschland. Ein Tagebuch 1955–1999* [Men and Masks: Art and Politics in East Germany; A Diary, 1955–99].

INKOTA: An ecumenical network of development-policy grassroots organizations, shops and church communities, which understands itself as part of the worldwide globalization-critical movement. Christa Wolf was a member of its advisory committee.

Ellen and Jörg Jannings: Jörg Jannings (born 1930), radio play director, headed the Artistic Word department at RIAS until 1993. In 1997 he directed a radio play based on Christa Wolf's *Medea* for NDR. A friend of Christa and Gerhard Wolf.

Aenne and Frieder Schlotterbeck: Friedrich Schlotterbeck (1909–79), writer; spent ten years in concentration camps and prisons under National Socialism for illegal antifascist resistance as a communist, escaped to Switzerland in 1944. He and his wife Anna Schlotterbeck (1902–72) moved to East Germany in 1948. In the GDR, the two of them were again sentenced to imprisonment in the course of Stalinist trials. Christa and Gerhard Wolf were friends of theirs until their deaths.

Raya and Lev Kopelev: Lev Kopelev (1912–97), Russian Germanist and writer; rehabilitated in 1957 after political imprisonment, excluded from the CPSU in 1968 and discriminated against; left for Cologne in 1980, expatriated in 1981. Raya (Raissa Davydovna Orlova-Kopelev, 1918–89), Americanist and writer; second wife of Lev Kopelev, expatriated from the Soviet Union along with him in 1981. Both were friends with Christa and Gerhard Wolf since 1965.

Otl Aicher and Inge Aicher-Scholl: Otl Aicher (1922–91) and his wife Inge Aicher-Scholl (1917–2000) met Christa and Gerhard Wolf in 1987 at the awarding of the Geschwister Scholl Prize to Christa Wolf and remained in very good contact.

Efim Etkind (1918–99): Russian literary scholar and translator; defended Alexander Solzhenitsyn and Joseph Brodsky; excluded from the Soviet Union in 1974, he taught at the Université Paris X Nanterre for many years. A friend of Christa and Gerhard Wolf.

Correspondence with Anna Seghers: Anna Seghers and Christa Wolf, *Das dicht besetzte Leben. Briefe, Gespräche und Essays* [The Densely Occupied Life: Letters, Conversations and Essays] (Angela Drescher ed.) (Berlin: Aufbau Verlag, 2003).

Correspondence with Charlotte Wolff: Christa Wolf and Charlotte Wolff, *Ja, unsere Kreise berühren sich* [Yes, Our Circles Touch] (Munich: Luchterhand Literaturverlag, 2004).

2004

Carlfriedrich Claus (1930–98): Avant-garde artist, known internationally for his *Sprachblätter*; a friend of Christa and Gerhard Wolf from 1970. Numerous titles on Claus have been published by the Gerhard Wolf Janus press, Berlin, including *Zwischen dem Einst und dem Einst. Sprachblätter 1959–1993* [Between Once and Once: Language Folios, 1959–93] (1993) and *Aurora* (1995); an enlargement of these sheets is on display in the German parliament.

Gerald J. Trageiser (born 1942): Head of Luchterhand Literaturverlag from 1995 to 2004, Christa Wolf's then publisher.

'The part of Brigitte Reimann . . .': Martina Gedeck played the role of the writer in *Hunger auf Leben* [Hunger for Life], a film based on Brigitte Reimann's diaries and directed by Markus Imboden.

2005

'Kurt Stern's diary entries . . .' : Kurt Stern, *Was wird mit uns geschehen? Tagebücher der Internierung 1939 und 1940*

[What Will Happen to Us? Internment Diaries, 1939 and 1940], with a foreword by Christa Wolf (Berlin: Aufbau Verlag, 2006. Kurt Stern (1907–89), a writer, moved to East Berlin with his wife Jeanne Stern (1908–2000) in 1946, after fighting against Francisco Franco's forces in the Spanish Civil War and subsequent exile in Mexico. Friends of Christa and Gerhard Wolf.

'The catalogue of the Carlfriedrich Claus exhibition . . .' : The exhibition *Schrift. Zeichen. Geste. Carlfriedrich Claus im Kontext von Klee bis Pollock* [Script, Signs, Gestures: Carlfriedrich Claus in Context from Klee to Pollock] was shown at the Kunstsammlungen Chemnitz from 24 July to 9 October 2005. The catalogue of the same name (Ingrid Mössinger and Brigitta Milde ed.) (Cologne: Wienand, 2005) contains Christa Wolf's essay 'An Carlfriedrich Claus erinnern' [Remembering Carlfriedrich Claus]. Also available in: Christa Wolf, *Rede, daß ich dich sehe. Essays, Reden, Gespräche* [Speak, So as to See You: Essays, Speeches, Conversations] (Berlin: Suhrkamp Verlag, 2012), pp. 131f.

Christoph Stölzl (born 1944): journalist and former director of the German Historical Museum in Berlin, co-presented the RBB television show *Im Palais* in 2004–05.

2006

'An essay by Dietmar Dath . . .' : Dietmar Dath, 'Science-fiction in nüchternen Versen', *Frankfurter Allgemeine*, 27 September 2006. Available at: https://goo.gl/-jP0hhy (last accessed on 17 February 2017).

'Poetics lectures that Peter Bichsel held . . .': Peter Bichsel, *Der Leser. Das Erzählen: Frankfurter Poetik-Vorlesungen*

[The Reader. The Telling: The Frankfurt Lectures on Poetics] (Frankfurt am Main: Suhrkamp Verlag, 1997[1982]), p. 83ff.

DARE: Democracy and Human Rights Education in Europe; Katrin Wolf supported this network during its first three years in existence.

'George Steiner's book . . .': George Steiner, 'Ten (Possible) Reasons for the Sadness of Thought', *Salmagundi* 146–7 (Spring–Summer 2005): 3–32; here, p. 3. Available at: https://goo.gl/euDihv (last accessed on 17 February 2017). Published in book form in German translation as *Warum Denken traurig macht. Zehn (mögliche) Gründe* (Frankfurt am Main: Suhrkamp Verlag, 2006).

2007

'Hanjo Kesting has sent a book . . .': Hanjo Kesting, *Begegnungen mit Hans Mayer: Aufsätze und Gespräche* [Encounters with Hans Mayer: Essays and Conversations] (Göttingen: Wallstein Verlag, 2007), p. 91.

Cornelius Schnauber (born 1939): Professor of German studies at the University of Southern California in Los Angeles. Publications include *Spaziergänge durch das Hollywood der Emigranten* [Walks through the Emigrants' Hollywood] (1992).

Nuria Quevedo (born 1938): Painter and graphic artist of Catalonian origin, who went into exile in Berlin with her parents in 1952; since 1997, she has spent part of the year in the Catalan Sant Feliu de Guíxols. Her close friendship with Christa Wolf began in the 1980s during her work on etchings to accompany *Cassandra*.

2009

Die Linke: The Left, also commonly referred to as the Left Party, is a democratic-socialist populist political party in Germany, which was founded in 2007 with the merger of the Party of Democratic Socialism (PDS) and the Electoral Alternative for Labour and Social Justice (WASG).

FDP: The Free Democratic Party is a liberal and classical liberal political party in Germany. It was a junior coalition partner in Angela Merkel's CDU-led coalition government from 2009 to 2013.

Honza's book: Jan Faktor, *Georgs Sorgen um die Vergangenheit oder Im Reich des heiligen Hodensack-Bimbams von Prag* [Major Concerns for the Past or In the Realm of the Holy Scrotum Bimbam of Prague] (Cologne: Kiepenheuer & Witsch, 2010).

'A book from Gerhard Begrich . . .': Gerhard Begrich, *Schönheit gilt es zu schauen: Theologie und Poesie* [Beauty Must Be Seen: Theology and Poetry] (Stuttgart: Radius Verlag, 2010). The title of the essay on Christa Wolf translates as 'What Remains. The Quest for Christa Wolf'.

2011

Book about [Estela Canto's] relationship to Borges: Estela Canto, *Borges im Gegenlicht*, (Christian Hansen trans.) (Munich: Kunstmann Antje, 1998). Originally: *Borges a contraluz* [Borges in Counterlight] (Madrid: Espasa Calpe, 1989).